# CAN WE MANAGE TO SAVE HEALTHCARE?

# Can We Manage to Save Healthcare?

## Lessons From the Zombie (Coronavirus) Apocalypse

George R. Cybulski, MD, MBA

Copyright © 2024 by George R. Cybulski

ISBN-13: 978-1-942389-29-3

All rights reserved. No part of this book may be reproduced or transmitted in any form or by any means without written permission from the author.

Edited by Writer Services, LLC.
Cover Design and Book Layout by Writer Services, LLC.

Prominent Books and the Prominent Books logo are Trademarks of Prominent Books, LLC.

# Table of Contents

**Dedication** ............................................................. xiii

**Disclaimer** ............................................................. xv

**Foreword** ............................................................... 1

**Introduction** ........................................................... 3

**Chapter One**
The Post-Pandemic Apocalypse State of Patient Care ........ 7

**Chapter Two**
What Killed the Healing Arts? ........................................ 11
    Technology Intrudes on the Patient–Care Provider
    Relationship ............................................................ 13

**Chapter Three**
Hospital Business Models—
From the Doctor's Workshop to the Firm to Hotels and
Food Courts ............................................................... 15
    So, Where Does That Leave Hospitals Today?
    Too Big to Fail? ........................................................ 27

**Chapter Four**
Management of Patient Care: Barbarians at the Gate...... 29

**Chapter Five**
The Blind Leading the Deaf:
The Frontline, Skin in the Game, and Monday-Morning Quarterbacks.................................................................... 35

**Chapter Six**
The Health Care Executive Pyramid .................................. 41
    Table One ............................................................................46

**Chapter Seven**
Why Ignoring the Coming Obsolescence of Hospitals is Holding Health Care Equality Back..................................... 49

**Chapter Eight**
The Word Salad That Dominates Our Health Care .......... 57

**Chapter Nine**
Obamacare: Solving the Wrong Problem Precisely or The Law of Unintended Consequences...................................... 65
    The Power of Fallacies........................................................69

**Chapter Ten**
Health Care Economics Part 1:
Survivorship Bias, a Scottish Professor, and the Visible Hand................................................................ 73
    The Cult of Management:
    False Gods and the Visible Hand ..........................................80

**Chapter Eleven**
Health Care Consultants:
Eating the Brains of the Living?.......................................... 87

**Chapter Twelve**
We Have Met the Enemy, and They are Us! ...... 93
    Transformation of Power .................................................. 101

**Chapter Thirteen**
The Pandemic Disruption of Health Care ...................... 105

**Chapter Fourteen**
Trust Me, Everybody's Doing It! The Reality of Consumer-Driven Health Care ............................................................ 109

**Chapter Fifteen**
Health Care Transformation:
Brutal Facts of Health Care's Pandemic "Creative Destruction" and Why Innovation of Patient Care is so Challenging ........................................................................ 113
    Bureaucracy ........................................................................ 114
    Health Insurance ............................................................... 114
    Markets and Value ............................................................. 114
    Leadership ......................................................................... 115
    Creative Destruction ......................................................... 116
    The Medical–Industrial Complex
    (Andrew "Bud" Relman, M.D.) ......................................... 118

**Chapter Sixteen**
The Failure of Public Health and Federal Health Agency Administration .................................................................. 121

**Chapter Seventeen**
It's Time for Health Care "Leaders" to Take Their Medicine ............................................................................ 127

## Chapter Eighteen
The "Invisible Hand" and the Dysfunctional Market of Health Care .................................................................................... 135
  Dysfunctional Health Care Markets ................................. 139
  Consumer-Driven Health Care .......................................... 140

## Chapter Nineteen
Dominant Forces in Health Care Management:
The Halo Effect ..................................................................... 143
  Trust and Leadership ........................................................... 146
  The Halo Effect of Leadership ........................................... 146
  Sophisms ................................................................................ 148
  Power Does Not Equal Leadership ................................... 150

## Chapter Twenty
Ghost Leadership and Zombie Management of
Health Care ........................................................................... 155
  The "Visible Hand" of Management in Health Care Organizations ....................................................................... 158

## Chapter Twenty-One
Strategy in Health Care: What is it and Why So Complicated? ....................................................................... 161

## Chapter Twenty-Two
Lessons of the Pandemic: The Price of Panic ................... 169

## Chapter Twenty-Three
Dumbing Down Health Care ............................................. 175
  Will the Amazonians Take Over Health Care? ............... 178

**Chapter Twenty-Four**
What Would Success in Health Care Reform
Even Look Like?................................................................. 181
    The COVID Pandemic Has Changed Patient Care Forever!
    (If we will only accept that!) ............................................... 183

**Chapter Twenty-Five**
Diagnosis and Cure: The Business Transformation of
American Medicine............................................................ 185
    The Cure: Table 2 .................................................................. 187
    New Economics of Health Care ........................................... 188
    Restoring Value to Health Care ........................................... 189

**Chapter Twenty-Six**
Value/Quality/Cost/Efficiency: Are We Measuring the
Critical Needs of Patient Care?......................................... 191
    The Value Paradox................................................................. 192
    What is the Quality of Quality Measurement? ................. 193
    Value........................................................................................ 194
    Value-Based Health Care: A Critical Examination........... 197

**Chapter Twenty-Seven**
Calling On All "Doctors of Humanity" ........................... 199
    "Doctors of Humanity" ........................................................ 200
    Table 3: Economic Targets for Optimizing Decision-
    Making in Patient Care......................................................... 201

**Chapter Twenty-Eight**
The Dysfunctional Health Care Market ........................... 203

**Chapter Twenty-Nine**
It's Crunch Time for Health Care ..................................... 207

**Chapter Thirty**
The "Unended" Quest ....................................................... 209

**Conclusion** ........................................................................ 211

**About the Author** ........................................................... 215

**Bibliography** ................................................................... 217
    Essential References ................................................... 218
    Further Reading of Interest ....................................... 231
    Academic References ................................................. 235

# Dedication

This book is the result of many, many people who have supported the privilege I have been fortunate to have in being a practitioner of the healing arts. My supporters include my family and friends, my teachers and mentors, and the patients who have placed their faith and trust in me. To all of them, I dedicate this book as a reflection of my commitment in kind to them.

# Disclaimer

The information in this book is presented to the best of the author's knowledge and for informational purposes only. It is not intended to be a substitute for professional or medical advice. The author and publisher make no representations or warranties of any kind, express or implied, about the completeness, accuracy, reliability, suitability, or availability with respect to the information contained in this book. Any reliance you place on such information is strictly at your own risk.

The author and publisher disclaim any liability for any loss or damage, including without limitation, indirect or consequential loss or damage, or any loss or damage whatsoever arising from the use or misuse of the information provided in this book. It is recommended to consult with a qualified professional or medical practitioner before making any decisions or taking any actions based on the information in this book.

The inclusion of any links, resources, or references in this book does not necessarily imply a recommendation or endorsement by the author or publisher. The author and publisher shall not be responsible for the content, accuracy, or availability of any external websites or resources mentioned in this book.

Every effort has been made to ensure that the information in this book is accurate and up to date at the time of publication. However, the author and publisher do not warrant or guarantee the accuracy, reliability, or completeness of the information, and they shall not be held responsible for any errors or omissions.

The views and opinions expressed in this book are those of the author and do not necessarily reflect the official policy or position of any organization, institution, or individual mentioned in the book.

# Foreword

In 2020–2021 an event, the Covid-19 pandemic, occurred for which the health care systems of the world were little prepared. In its aftermath, health care barely survived. Yes, the physical structures of hospitals and clinics appear unchanged as nurses, doctors, physician assistants, etc. go about the process of patient care, but these hospital buildings and activities hide a fragile enterprise. Today, many more people continue to suffer from the lingering effects of the Covid-19 pandemic —whether it be "long Covid" sequelae of infection of the cardiorespiratory system or the brain, or whether it be the burnout of the nurses, doctors, and staff who were on the front-line of infection futilely witnessing the deadly effects of the coronavirus.

However, others such as the political, business, academic, hospital, and health care organization executives who were never actually on the pandemic frontline survived unscathed but remain infected by another type of malady that further puts in peril the survival of health care. Like the mythological undead creatures that live following an apocalypse, these "zombies" are infected with a "disease" of the mind if you will —that of conventional thinking, groupthink and resistance to innovation in the United States and the world that makes health care delivery fraught with inequity of access, safety, quality, and efficiency.

The heroic example and sacrifice of all who were on the frontlines of the pandemic must be honored by dedication to efforts free of the biases of self-interest that are an ongoing plague of health care and that have gutted it of its ability to adapt and find solutions for inequity.

Unless we *manage* to change health care, we might not be so lucky with the next pandemic. To all those who have made such a great sacrifice during the Covid-19 pandemic, this book is dedicated with the aim of awakening the effort needed to save health care.

# Introduction

The story of health care is that of a vast *War and Peace* type saga of an industry composed of millions and millions of stories of people seeking help or relief from suffering to make their lives better and more prosperous.

These stories of providing care for preserving or restoring health or for having a peaceful death involve every part of society including governmental, legal, charitable, educational, and business organizations.

As such, we are all involved every day, whether directly or indirectly, in the care of each other.

These stories display the full range of human emotion and effort from the most romantic, idealistic, and heroic to the most commonplace, selfish, and venal.

Because health care spans such a broad array of organizational and emotional involvement, there are many entry points for all of us to interact or participate in health care.

This is a story that includes idealism and commitment, the healing arts and the struggle to provide the best patient care, analysis with dismay of the barriers to equity in health care, and the hope of overcoming those obstacles and sustaining the ideals of the healing arts for the care of the sick and for the betterment of humanity.

I find myself, after forty years as a doctor, in the circumstance of bringing specialty surgical care to patients with a safety-net hospital whose mission is "advancing health equity." In this regard, as one of my like-minded former colleagues, doctor Nader Dahdaleh, would say to me, "it's a pleasure to serve."

However, my forty years have also witnessed changes in providing care with a more and more intrusive nature of business and politics interposed in the relationship between patient and doctor.

The art of medicine is traditionally comprised of creating an atmosphere of trust and commitment that eludes metrics and surveys, and certainly enhancement by the electronic medical record. Nonetheless, the shift in health care delivery involves more and more business practices, management, and politics, creating an imbalance in which more and more of the expenditure on health care in the United States goes toward administrative bureaucracy and technology that is by default a boondoggle to business but a bane to patient care.

Politicians of the mentality to "pass anything" in order to support their voters' special health care interests put unrealistic demands and expectations on a delivery system that is handicapped in meeting those promises. Consequently, the system of health care is rigged by those who use it to provide services to their advantage.

Despite over four trillion dollars spent on health care in the United States alone, the unevenness of morbidity and mortality regionally across our country remains unresolved. The principal factors behind this inequity of health include the economics of the "medical–industrial complex," political expediency, and other aspects of self-interest.

Inequity of health occurs not only in access to health care services but supporting factors of health such as diet, working conditions, education, etc.

The pandemic exposed the culpability of the zombie executives insulated by the health care bureaucracies they occupy from adapting to the pandemic crisis.

*"That's the thing about zombies. They don't adapt, and they don't think."*

—*Max Brooks*

# Chapter One

## The Post-Pandemic Apocalypse State of Patient Care

*"We cannot solve our problems with the same thinking we used when we created them."*

—Albert Einstein

The Covid-19 pandemic of 2020–2023 posed an existential threat to public health. It also exposed long-standing trouble in the relationship between health care practitioners and the management and administrative aspects of the health care delivery system. These troubles, which have been brewing for years, were the consequence of government policies and business interests that left out the frontline of care providers from leadership and management of hospitals, clinics, etc. In fact, the various government programs that fund health care, combined with a dysfunctional marketplace, created friction that distracted from focus on quality, safety, and efficiency of patient care. It also produced waste and huge opportunities for fraud and abuse. Even health care managers with good intentions struggle to navigate the complex and out-dated organizational structure of health care delivery, that of a pyramid with those at the top in executive positions extracting value under the guise of providing leadership. In this pyramid of health care delivery organizations, the role of nurses and physicians as leaders in hospitals and clinics has been subject to greater and greater oversight of professional managers and executives. This power grab has produced a conflict between hospitals and their nurses and physicians over the very soul of the healing arts.

The hierarchical system of health care management and executive positions has been fashioned into pyramid-like structures based on the typical business organization. As with any business structure, the support base is large, and it gradually narrows as it reaches the top, where the compensation for executives is abundantly higher. These health care hierarchical pyramids are the opposite of Maslow's Pyramid, which is a model for personal development. The health care management pyramid includes functions such as finance and human resources, which have little to no direct contact with patients and lack of humanitarian qualities. The use of resources for executive compensation packages is a drain on critical components of patient care and the ability to invest in it. This was the stage upon which the existential threat of the Covid-19 pandemic entered.

During the pandemic, nurses, doctors, and their support teams heroically stepped into the breach to care for patients afflicted with a deadly, here-to-fore, little-understood opponent, often without basic personal protective equipment. This occurred despite the fact that we live in the wealthiest country in the world with the most spent per person on health care as well. Who can ever forget the images of health care workers wearing black garbage bags tending to coronavirus patients? The pandemic has figuratively and literally forced the harsh light of day on the facade of this system. How did this inexcusable state occur?

The shortages of basic equipment during the pandemic were a result of a failure in the health care supply chain that had been developing for years. Hospital management has tightened control over suppliers for patient care by implementing cost-cutting techniques, such as lean supply chain practices borrowed from other industries, which can have dire consequences in the health care setting. These practices, modeled after just-in-time automobile assembly line production, do not align with the requirements for patient care that should at least exceed these minimal standards.

This failure of the health care supply chain highlights the disconnect between the front-line health care providers and the bureaucracy that has become a standard in the "medical–industrial complex," referred to by Dr. Arnold Reman in 1980.

The bureaucracies that support the provision of patient care are vast and numerous. Who are the types that more and more occupy these bureaucracies? They are not domain knowledge workers from actual patient care training but MBAs, lawyers, business people, etc. They don't innovate either because they are too risk averse and lack the knowledge of the process of providing health services and the value of the patient relationship. Can we manage to save health care from the grips of the business mindset and political dysfunction of governmental bureaucracies that have infected it?

We can. We must!

## Chapter Two

## What Killed the Healing Arts?

*"It's time to return to the emphasis on patients first and restore the true purpose of the healing arts."*

—George Cybulski, Neurosurgery

While I was taking care of patients over the past forty years, the healing arts of nursing and medicine became a business called "health care." How do we measure this change? How has health care as a business performed? Is access to health care today worth the price? Does the reality of health care match the expectations?

Popular television shows like *Grey's Anatomy, The Resident, The Good Doctor, New Amsterdam,* and others often portray doctors and nurses as compassionate and heroic figures. Similarly, hospitals are often depicted as places of refuge and care, where chief medical officers (CMOs) will break any rule for the benefit of a patient, standing up for what is fair and just, and heroically advocating for saving lives, at any cost. It's interesting to see decades of longrunning shows with idyllic themes of doctors having the power to fully care for their patients, and one can only assume that the populous either believes that this is what health care is or, at least, someone wants the people to think it's this way.

The reality is that the CMOs and chief nursing officers (CNOs) of most hospitals are primarily responsible for administrative tasks tied to regulatory functions removed from direct patient care. They act as a liaison between the medical and nursing staff and the hospital's executives, who usually have a business background rather than a medical one. While CMOs and CNOs may help to explain the complexities of patient care to the executives, they often have little influence on the overall business decisions and management of the hospital.

As hospitals have become increasingly more complex to manage due to burgeoning regulations from federal, state, and local governments, the connection between administration and front-line delivery of health care becomes more and more tenuous. Resources necessary for meeting regulatory requirements drain away investment from equipment and services that would directly benefit patient care.

The business focus of hospitals is pernicious. In order to offset revenue lost on meeting regulatory standards, hospitals have adopted other profit tactics. For example, primary care doctors are often excluded from the care of their own patients whom they admit to the hospital by hospitalists. This new subspecialty of medicine generates income for the hospitals as these physicians are employed or contracted by the hospitals and work on shifts. These hospitalists see the patients of primary care doctors and manage their care. This prevents family doctors from managing their own patients. When these patients are discharged from the hospital, the hospitalist has no further contact with them. This is a far cry from what is being portrayed to the masses.

Accordingly, the hospitalist model raises several questions about the priority of care over profit. To whom are the shift-working hospitalists accountable: the patient or the hospital? Can a doctor who has never met a patient before provide the same degree of care as the patient's family doctor who has known the patient for many years? Patients would likely prefer a doctor they know and trust rather than one they have never met before. Patient opinion aside, this needs to be further discussed from a medical perspective. Is there any wonder that the trust of patients in the health care "system" is diminishing? This is also linked to inequity of access, safety, and quality of patient care that pervades medical care.

## Technology Intrudes on the Patient–Care Provider Relationship

In the interest of increasing productivity and improving the efficiency of delivery, political/governmental agencies and health care management have embraced the electronic medical record (EMR) as a way to streamline patient/nurse/physician interactions. However, the simple fact of inserting a computer screen between a care provider and a patient actually creates barriers to the opportunity to engage on a human level. Nonetheless, EMRs, which are nothing more than glorified record-keeping apparatuses, are valued more for their capture of billing than for patient care.

The ever-expanding control of the "health care–industrial complex" spurred on by economic self-interest, comes at the sacrifice of empathy, clinical decision-making skills, and other intangible, undervalued benefits to patient care.

The result is a vicious circle of increased stress for care providers. The healing arts have become more of an assembly line process, and as a result, the caring aspect of health care is increasingly compromised. The result is an unhealthy environment for patient care, and this began before the coronavirus struck.

Pandemic aside, the health care systems of the United States and the world have lost touch with their core mission of providing compassionate care. As a physician with over forty years of patient care experience, I have seen firsthand not only the detrimental effects but also the more terrifying and dehumanizing nature of those who control health care. In this book, we lay out the diagnosis surrounding the takeover of the healing arts by business interests and explore the treatment critical to reclaiming the focus on providing the best possible patient care.

It's time to return to the emphasis on patients first and restore the true purpose of health care.

## Chapter Three

## Hospital Business Models— From the Doctor's Workshop to the Firm to Hotels and Food Courts

*"The firm is dead; long live the firm...."*
—Arman A. Alchian and Susan Woodward (Economists)

Over forty-five years ago, I had my first professional exposure to hospitals as an idealistic medical student in rural central Illinois. My awe of the amazing things I saw happening in that community hospital so impressed me that I was hooked on the magnificence of hospitals and their vital role in patient care. While understandingly very naïve at that time, I marveled as the surgeon with whom I was assigned, who worked constantly from patient to patient, performing procedures, speaking with other doctors, and continuously helping patients.

Subsequently, I was very fortunate during my own surgical training in the early 1980s to be continuously at work seeing patients in the ER, assisting in surgery, and doing bedside procedures while studying and absorbing knowledge like a proverbial sponge. I was also so fortunate to have old-school doctors as role models during this time. I contrast my hospital learning experiences with those a few decades later when I observed my own residents working as data entry clerks, pecking away at the electronic medical record (EMR) instead of learning at the bedside as Dr. Osler had laid out as the foundation of medical training in the early 1900s.

I loved hospitals and what we could do to help people in them, and until about 1999, hospitals loved my efforts back. As my principal "workshop" began to transform to become more like a hotel than a cathedral of healing, I should have seen the proverbial handwriting, or at least the artwork, on the wall.

Why did this change? As with any other business, the use of marketing took hold, along with the financial management of hospitals. While technological advances in diagnosis and therapeutics moved patient care dramatically forward, the expense of technology for patient care requiring significant capital investment made the hospital the controller of the physician's efforts.

As Karl Marx asked, "Who controls the means of production…?" I don't want to get too Marxian, but Marx had a point in his book *Capital: A Critique of Political Economy*, which has relevance to the current situation in health care. Karl Marx wrote that controlling the means of production in any given industry ultimately dictates control over labor. When applied to the health care industry, which is increasingly being run as a business, there is a battle for control between those who prioritize healing and care for patients and those who prioritize profits and business interests.

Hospitals, as repositories of expensive technology (MRI scanners, hi-tech ORs, etc.) control the means of production, especially in my specialty of neurosurgery. Hospitals are run by businesspeople, and de facto business controls production.

As Jeff Bezos put it, "Do we own the process, or does the process own us?" Thus, the strategic objectives are no different for providing health services as a $4 trillion "prize" (McKinsey[1]) that offers many opportunities for business types to enter the market, dysfunctional as it is.

The takeover and stranglehold of hospital management was subtle and gradual, like a python slowly extinguishing its prey. While my love of hospitals persists today, as does my appreciation for the miracles that occur in hospitals, things are no longer the same, and much of what health care was all about originally—care of the sick as the primary goal—has been obscured.

My nostalgia is about those good ole days when "patients first" was more than a marketing slogan. The shifting of hospitals away from the true essence of care is tragic. There is no secret to caring for the patient. It is simply caring for the patient (Peabody[2]).

---

[1] Refers to a concept introduced by a prominent management consulting firm, McKinsey & Company, a decade ago, describing value-based care as a potential "prize" worth $4 trillion in enterprise value.

[2] Francis Peabody delivered a seminal speech in 1926 to medical students at Harvard University emphasizing essential qualities of clinicians, including the allocation of time, sympathy, and understanding to patients. He underscored the personal bond formed between physicians and patients as the true reward of medical practice and stressed the significance of cultivating an interest in the humanity of patients.

My main hospital of practice for over thirty years (excluding service in the US Army Medical Corps in Operation Desert Shield/Desert Storm) emphasized its illusory recognition of the irrelevant United States News and World Report survey as a "Best Hospital." Myself, I would prefer the best nurses and doctors. The amount of dollars diverted from patient care, spent on marketing in the name of branding, raises questions as to where the motives of health care executives lie. Should branding be so important as to affect the level of supply stocks at less than optimum levels (as was seen with masks, gloves, and gowns during the Covid pandemic)?

While I still am fortunate to experience the commitment of like-minded nurses, nurses' aids, medical students and residents, techs, unit clerks, orderlies (I prefer this old-school name over "transporters"), cleaning women/men, and numerous others committed to performing the gifts of caring for people, the reciprocal love from hospitals run by business and political people has disappeared.

The commoditization of care, like any other type of business, is the reality of today as hospitals have become enfolded into larger and larger systems requiring concomitant management structures that run these "big boxes" like other big box businesses.

Although Canada has given us my favorite sport, ice hockey, it has also provided two men—one favored and the other not-so-favored to me—who have had a substantial impact on the management of the hierarchies of patient care and consequently the business of health care in the United States.

One is Malcolm MacEachern (1881–1956), an obstetrician-gynecologist whose legacy is the takeover of hospital hierarchy by accountants, lawyers, and MBAs. Accordingly, these are executives who rarely have had any direct patient care experience.

As such, they combine a business model of financial management with an unquenchable thirst for power that would be familiar to Napoleon.

The other Canadian is Professor Henry Mintzberg, a professor of management studies at McGill University, Montreal, who consistently has dedicated his work to unraveling the inefficiencies of management hierarchies—more on that later.

As it were, MacEachern won the race for heading the American College of Surgeons (ACS) Hospital Standardization Program and handed it over to the "professional" administrators who hold sway today.

The original leader of the ACS Hospital Standardization Program was a Boston surgeon named Ernest Amory Codman (1869–1940). Aside from pioneering work in anesthesiology, general surgery, orthopedic surgery, and radiology, Dr. Codman created measures for outcomes of hospital treatment. Dr. Codman even started his own hospital for teaching these results—way ahead of his time.

Hospitals used to embody a sense of devotion to the goal of healing the sick, but as hospital bureaucracies have expanded, the focus on this mission has shifted toward business functions. This has led to a decline in the perception of hospitals as sacred places of healing. Furthermore, as hospitals continue merging into larger systems, they become corporations that take on the character and behavior of other types of non-health care-related corporations. As such, health care systems replicate corporate news from other industries of outrageous CEO salaries and record annual net income on their investment portfolios. Case in point: "Kaiser sets new record for annual net income of $8.1B" —*Healthcare Dive*, 2/14/2022.

Experience in the professions of nursing and medicine counts for something. Actually, it counts for everything. It conveys the trust and commitment that is the essence of the healing arts. It is gained through the activity of taking care of patients day and night, and learning what works, none of which is easily replaceable.

Over time, I have observed the development of detachment of the managers and executives in these bureaucracies, with more and more expansion of the executive suite required to cope with regulatory and financial aspects of health care as a business rather than the original mission of providing healing in a health care facility. Business supplants humanity.

To be fair to my few dedicated hospital executive colleagues, regulatory red tape alone makes hospitals "the most complex human organization ever devised," as noted by management guru Peter Drucker, a journalist by training, who created a portfolio not in terms of companies that he actually saved but in regard to expressing a humanistic perspective on the management challenges facing all types of organizations, including hospitals.

Apparently, on such an engagement for a hospital, Drucker began his analysis with the deconstruction of the hospital's mission statement. For Drucker, the mission statement dictates both the objective and the means to obtain it. In an article by Rahul Vitekar, "Peter Drucker- Why does Emergency Room in a hospital exist? Brilliant!" the author states that Drucker's words are a great reminder of never taking the mission of any organization or any organizational unit for granted, and that Drucker's clarity in defining mission statements is a testament to his genius. Vitekar also writes that the clarity and coherence of Drucker's mission statement for the hospital's emergency room is an example of how defining a mission can reconcile the role and mission of a unit within the larger role and mission of an organization. "A mission statement has to be operational; otherwise it's just good intentions."—Drucker[3]

That is the opposite of where we find ourselves with the "businessification" and political influence on the healing arts today!

Nonprofit hospitals have difficulty justifying their exemption from state and federal taxes by providing enough community benefits in the form of care for Medicaid patients and charity care[4].

Maybe their advertising campaigns are targeting the wrong audience (sarcasm intended).

The political factor plays a significant role in exacerbating the unequal distribution of health care services. The building of hospitals in the United States was fostered by politicians through laws such as the Hill-Burton Act of 1946 and the Hospital Survey and Construction Act. Although these laws were enacted with the intention of addressing the disparities

---

[3] From the book *Managing the Non-Profit Organization: Principles and Practices*, by Peter F. Drucker; HarperCollins.

[4] From the 2022 article, "Evaluation of Unreimbursed Medicaid Costs Among Nonprofit and For-Profit US Hospitals" by Ge Bai, PhD, CPA1; Hossein Zare, PhD, MS; and David A. Hyman, MD, JD.

in health care access for the poor, they have had the unintended result of further exacerbating inequalities in health care delivery, with expansion of the business and legal-trained individuals filling the positions of health care management.

Politics can be even more perverse when it comes to health care.

As a medical student, I was fortunate enough to witness the advent of CT scanning, and by the time I completed my neurosurgical training in 1986, MRI scanning was already in use. Despite the tremendous advancements in patient care, I still see evidence of medical inequality in my current practice as a physician in one of the few remaining "safety-net" hospitals in Chicago. The obstacles that contribute to ongoing medical inequality are associated with third-party review.

Contrast this with the fact that within a few miles of my clinic, there are three major hospitals replete with the latest technology and trained staffing. Still, access to these medical marvels might as well be on the moon for most of my patients. The Covid pandemic only heightened the challenges for my patients as well as others whose diagnoses and treatments were delayed. According to NPR, Americans' health is deteriorating as the Omicron variant delays various medical procedures, including heart surgery and cancer treatment.[5]

Subsidized health insurance and Medicaid eligibility expansion (Obamacare) should have made health care more accessible and decreased inequality. In reality, Obamacare brought significant new business to commercial insurance companies—the gatekeepers of access to health care. As

---

5 Article "Americans get sicker as omicron stalls everything from heart surgeries to cancer care" February 4, 2022 by Will Stone.

reported in the Lex column of *The Financial Times* in March 2022, the "Big Five" insurers—United Health, Anthem, Cigna, Humana, and CVS Health (formerly Aetna) scored a record $33.1 billion in profit. All the while, I assist my patients by interacting (including faxing patient records and forms) with insurance middlemen to get their medications, tests, and surgeries approved. It has become a check-box, cook-book world in patient care today.

Former "public" health care systems have fallen in line. For example in 2002, one of the largest and most famous public hospitals in the United States had its replacement hospital named after a local politician, and its affiliated clinic named after one of its administration bureaucrats. Naming a public hospital after a local politician and its affiliated clinic after a bureaucrat is absurd and inappropriate. The absurdity of this tribute to politicians and bureaucratic functionaries is appalling in the context that previously, hospital buildings were named after medical and nursing pioneers. The focus of patient care has definitely changed.

The mission statements of hospitals have become nothing more than tag lines in slick marketing campaigns replete with meaningless advertising slogans. The inspiring and purposeful mission statements of nursing and medicine, which were centered on healing and comforting the sick, have been lost. Drucker highlighted the divide created by hospital strategies that prioritize business over patient care, stating that "there is only one definition of business purpose: to create a customer".[6] This is a striking reality as seen during the Covid-19 pandemic, where nurses, physicians, and other

---

[6] From the book, *Management: Tasks, Responsibilities, and Practices* by Peter F. Drucker; Harper Business.

health care workers on the frontlines worked tirelessly to provide care to those in need. As noted by Lisa Rosenbaum in "Harnessing Our Humanity – How Washington's Health Care Workers Have Risen to the Pandemic Challenge" in the *New England Journal of Medicine*, few hospital systems today have an advertising slogan that truly captures the essence of their mission. It's all about the marketing.

Health care administration has expanded to cope with regulations imposed by third-party payers, such as Medicare, along with having to conform to contracts with commercial insurance that affect all care providers (hospitals, clinics, physician offices, etc.). It is disturbing to see how the commercialization of health care has become an obstacle to the needs of the most vulnerable patients.

At what cost has the growth of this bureaucracy contributed to the inequality of health care by diverting funding for running the business function away from investment in patient care? Unfortunately, like other corporations, "big box" hospitals have no meaningful contact with their locale, and their executives are accountable only within the organizations and to their boards of directors.

The regulations and contracts put in place to manage medical care utilization and costs have led to an increase in administrative spending, reaching an estimated 25% of the total $3.8 billion spent on health care in 2019. Unfortunately, the attempts to control health care expenses have resulted in a vicious cycle of enlarging the administrative segment.

Hospitals used to be about relationships, but the growth of the administrative segment is principally about support of its own hierarchy. By some good fortune, I have been able to join the staff of a hospital that still values relationships and understands the value of doctors to their mission of excellent patient care. The big box hospitals where I have worked in the past have completely lost this perspective. Their focus on support of doctors and their patients has become secondary to their pursuit of political or business objectives.

This expansion contributes to the growing divide between administration, caregivers, and patients. This disconnection between the frontline health care providers and the financial and regulatory managers of hospitals detracts from the original mission and purpose of hospitals.

As hospitals own the "means of production" (Marx), they have tightened control over nurses and doctors.

However, as with the Stockholm Syndrome, in which prisoners come to love their captors, I still love hospitals and the true mission of the healing arts that has been fostered in conjunction with hospital development. I hold onto the romantic idea of hospitals as "doctors' workshops," but the reality is that the need for increased capital to pay for MRI/CT scanners, among other things, means that hospitals must operate as business entities, subject to economic realities such as return on investment and scarcity. This intrusion of economic considerations on physician behavior is expertly examined in Mark V. Pauly's book, specifically in Chapter 11.[7]

Ronald Coase's Nobel Prize-winning work *Theory of the Firm* (1991) also anticipated the transformation of hospital power. Coase theorized that businesses, or "firms," would emerge in areas where the transaction costs of production (in this case,

---

[7] *Doctors and Their Workshops* by Mark V. Pauly (ISBN 13: 9780226650449, published by University of Chicago Press in 1981)

for physicians in hospitals) necessitated an organization to handle these transactions, such as the provision of diagnostic equipment, supplies, and nursing support for surgery. Like Marx, Coase recognized that the excess value generated by production would accrue to the firm managing these transactions (in this case, the hospital). However, hospitals have increasingly taken more of this excess value and imposed anti-competitive practices on their medical staff that do little to increase the quality of the services they provide, to say nothing about its effect on morale.

The increased merger and acquisition activity of hospital systems in the United States from 2019 to 2021 has created a dysfunctional market effect. This has limited the options for physicians to join medical staffs and has protected incumbent hospitals from competition, potentially leading to negative consequences for health care providers and patients. Patients' access to their choice of caregiver is made by corporations.

One of the biggest conflicts of interest and anti-competitive behavior is in "teaching hospitals." Teaching hospitals or academic medical centers, which employ resident physicians in training, also employ medical school clinical faculty and have a symbiotic and financially crucial relationship with medical schools for their mutual benefit. Advertising by academic medical centers of their access to "clinical trials" and "translational" research engenders "hope" for patients with terrible afflictions.

The publication of Kocher, Shah, and Navathe titled *Overcoming the Market Dominance of Hospitals* (2021) highlights the impact of hospital consolidation and the rise of physician employment on health care delivery. The result is a concentration of physicians into large, business-like group practices.

This cascading trend puts more and more power in the hands of the richly rewarded executives of hospital systems who not only benefit from restriction of competition but who influence, both directly and indirectly, aspects of patient care; something that is disturbing, to say the least.

## So, Where Does That Leave Hospitals Today? Too Big to Fail?

While the rural community hospitals have never been more tenuous in terms of survival even prior to the pandemic, the enlarging hospital systems have continuously increased in size by pursuing a mergers and acquisitions strategy that has allowed them to reap the lion's share of the pandemic CARES Act dollars.

In the United States, by being mandated to be all health services to all people, hospitals are uneven—in terms of the quality, of those services provided—and it is just not possible to be excellent in all categories of medical care. The fantasy of this is unknown to the public and can result in tragic consequences.

The Covid-19 pandemic posed a significant challenge, leading to a high demand for ICU beds as operating rooms remained underutilized. The conversion of these beds showcased the adaptability of hospital management; however, the reduction in income from elective surgeries left many hospitals teetering on the edge. Without the infusion of CARES subsidies, these essential health care facilities would likely have also suffered the consequences of the pandemic.

Bartley J. Madden, a researcher on health care value and author of *The Pragmatic Theory of the Firm* and *Free to Choose*

*Medicine,* proposes a model for firms to better coordinate management and employees to create value. He emphasizes the importance of a firm being a "learning organization." The original concept of teaching hospitals aligned with this principle, but in recent times, their focus on business bureaucracy has overshadowed their original mission.

The division between hospital executives and frontline workers is significant. Communication in large hospitals is often structured and hierarchical, with a chain of command similar to the military. On occasion, the author has had conversations with hospital system CEOs and has noticed a disconnect in their perspectives on patient care. The CEO speaks in general terms and platitudes, while this surgeon and author operates at a process problem-solving level. The hospital hierarchical structure diffuses any suggestions for improving patient care, causing them to be diluted as they progress through committees. This rigid hierarchy can stifle any ability for adaptation in delivery processes.

Hospitals are such a prominent part of the care of patients, yet as they have become more business-centric in their focus, we have lost the intangibles that made them so critical in the approach to healing.

# Chapter Four

# Management of Patient Care: Barbarians at the Gate

The explosion of hospital hierarchy dominated by professionals who are accountants and MBAs. These executives rarely have direct clinical training. Consequently, they follow a business model of financial management and often an unquenchable thirst for power that makes Napoleon look like a rank amateur.

In the battle of the "suits" (accountants, MBAs, and business majors) versus the "scrubs" (nurses and doctors), the suits have won, and in hospitals, aside from the obligatory, regulatory-mandated Chief Nursing Officers and Chief Medical Officers, the "suits" dominate and hold tight control over all the purse strings for clinical departments and accordingly power over decision-making that directly affects people's lives. By the early 1970s, "the rise of health care" as a business was nearly complete.[8]

The ever-growing bureaucracy of health care demands the constant influx of newly minted, usually former frat boys and sorority sisters with health care management degrees to constantly fill the bottom of the pyramid and begin to master the skills as "yes-women" and "yes-men" in hopes that they can contribute enough toward buffing the image of their bosses to be promoted. Tragically, this has created a chasm between the executive offices and the frontline. The waste of time and resources better spent on improving patient care is siphoned off into meetings of management. The appeal of these positions has led to the fastest-growing segment of health care.

Administrative and management positions encompass the hierarchy of service support functions (e.g. finance, technology, supply chain, real estate, facility management staffing, human resources, etc.) Other functions like marketing, lobbying, and other soft brand-related positions divert money that could be better spent on patient care. Yet these "BS jobs" (Graeber[9]) proliferate in the business of health care, mimicking precisely the organization models of other types of business. Such jobs co-opt nurses and physicians by placating them with propaganda and promises that are rarely kept.

Today, nurses and physicians rarely hold executive positions of consequence in hospitals and hospital systems.

---

8 In reference to Gabriel Winant's book, *The Next Shift: The Fall of Industry and the Rise of Health Care Rust Belt America*, which promotes a shift from decommodified health care to corporate health. Congress and the President approved a major change from a labor-intensive, durational model of care, to a capital-intensive, interventionist model of treatment. Here was a pivotal point for the major transformation of health care.

9 Reference to the book, *Bullshit Jobs: A Theory* by David Graeber; Simon & Schuster 2018

The use of the retrospective scope (by which the standards of care dictate that all physicians are accountable to) does not apply to the professional class of management of hospitals. For example, have you ever heard of management malpractice? The only time I have ever encountered the concept was in an article in *The Wall Street Journal* ("Former Time Warner Chief Lashes Out at AT&T in Book," November 16, 2021) by Joe Flint. Former AT&T CEO Jeff Bewkes said regarding the merger with HBO that "we didn't think they would go to such a level of malpractice."

Hospital executives and managers are not responsible for patient care with the same diligence or accountability as nurses and doctors. Who are health care executives accountable to then? Unlike being subject to medical malpractice for nurses and physicians, management malpractice has no similar mechanism of scrutiny or accountability. There is no greater divergence between executives and the frontline than in this management of risk. Essentially, health care administration is insulated from the significant risks involved in patient care, such as the uncertainty, decision-making, and responsibility for outcomes.

The "risk" management departments in hospitals, which are staffed by lawyers and nurses, typically operate in a reactive manner, conducting post-facto analysis of medical treatments that did not meet expectations. Due to their limited knowledge of clinical matters, their main focus is "cover your ass" for the hospitals. The risks of patient care fall squarely on frontline caregivers who have to face consequences when unexpected clinical results occur. Outdated "risk management" is an indictment of health care organizations run by non-clinical executives and managers.

That's because principally hospitals, but also clinics, ambulatory care centers, etc., are more financial than clinical in their commitment. Most health care executives possess a huge blind spot in this regard. They possess no knowledge and skills required for providing patient care, including medical, nursing, and other clinical specialties. Domain knowledge of patient care requires rigorous study and dedication involving sacrifice that can't be duplicated in a business school course of study. (Because of my innate curiosity, I acquired an executive health care MBA and can speak from experience that while intellectually stimulating, it produced no redeeming health care quality revelations). Patient care is unique and demands special knowledge not transferable to accounting or finance.

In 2004, Henry Mintzberg wrote a book called *Managers Not MBAs*. In it, he critically evaluated those limitations of MBAs in the role of management.

The potential for value contribution to patient care from an MBA education, in its essence, involves economic decision-making weighing scarcity and tradeoffs. (Bernie Sanders proposed to provide unlimited vision, dental, and hearing through Medicare, despite its projected funding shortage in 2026.) However, these trade-offs are lost in translation. Since health care is now dominated by MBAs, there is a lack of both present and future thinking, and as such, health care is unsustainable.

The health care system's lack of sustainability is comparable to the financial crisis of 2008 as documented in *The Puritan Gift* (Hopper and Hopper, 2009), which becomes even more relevant in light of the health care crisis caused by the pandemic. As with the 2008 financial crisis, massive bailouts of hospitals were required to keep them afloat.

The leadership style of health care, dominated by MBAs, mirrors the arrogance and lack of foresight shown by banking industry executives leading up to the global financial crisis and depression of 2008–2010.

Just like the banks prior to the 2008–2010 financial crash, the health care industry has become "too big to fail," as evidenced by the increasing use of deficit spending via the CARES Act in the United States during the 2020–2021 pandemic crisis. Can the health care "bubble" continue to grow indefinitely without facing a similar collapse to the mortgage-backed securities bubble in 2008–2010?

# Chapter Five

# The Blind Leading the Deaf: The Frontline, Skin in the Game, and Monday-Morning Quarterbacks

The business of delivering health care is relevant to everyone. However, the current state of health care inequity raises questions about the priorities and capabilities of those running health care organizations. Are these politicians and business people primarily focused on financial efficiency or on politicians making promises that can't be kept? The bureaucratic nature of health care management, with its numerous layers of committees and arduous decision-making processes, often leads to focus on the wrong priorities. Unfortunately, the current state of hospital organization and management, and the regulations of third-party payers for health care is a hindrance to progress. It is characterized by a complex and slow system that fails to efficiently recognize and act on value propositions.

What administrators hear when physicians ask for new technology to enhance care of patients is "cost," "return on investment," "risk," etc. What physicians hear when administrators speak of seeing more patients, expenses, and the profit and bottom line is "cut corners and spend less time with patients." It's the blind (administrators) leading the deaf (health care providers).

That's due to the divide between those who provide direct patient care and the administrators who are primarily focused on managing the finance of that care. This division hinders the ability to produce value in health care, as it separates the individuals who are making critical decisions about patient care under stressful and uncertain conditions from those who engage in retrospective analysis and criticism.

The current state of health care management is hindered by a bureaucratic system that prioritizes financial expertise over clinical knowledge. Many health care executives, particularly those with MBA degrees, are trained in business and finance but lack a frontline perspective. This disconnect between the decision-makers controlling facilities and resources and those providing direct patient care creates barriers to the immediate needs of patients. Accordingly, medical professionals who are trained to make prompt and informed decisions, based on their clinical expertise, are hindered by the cumbersome hierarchical structure of the health care bureaucracy.

The difference in culture between health care management and health care practitioners affects collaboration and negatively impacts value due to a lack of mutual understanding and common language.

The depth to which lack of communication, wisdom, and judgment has sunk in patient care organizations cannot be bridged even by health care consultants (sarcasm intended). The old joke, from advertising executive Carl

Ally (1924–1999), that a consultant is someone who borrows your watch in order to tell you what time it is, still stands.

The book *The Puritan Gift: Reclaiming the American Dream Amidst Global Financial Chaos* by Hopper and Hopper examines the causes behind the financial crisis of 2007–2008 and highlights the difference between those who have practical experience and knowledge in managing a business and those who lack such expertise. This distinction was a critical factor in the banking industry during the 2008 crisis. The authors argue that domain knowledge, or knowledge and experience gained through experience and advancement within an industry, is important for effective management. However, the question arises whether this concept applies similarly to the health care industry.

For health care as a business, the same divide occurs. Unfortunately, it is worse because health care providers are taking care of a person's health despite the attempts to categorize diagnoses by codes and procedures as well. Business practices applied to patient care ignore the basic problem that people and their health conditions do not fit uniformly into diagnosis categories and determining the value of a health encounter cannot be expressed by formulas for the purpose of creating a bill for services. The healing arts are based on a relational encounter, while health care as a business is a transactional activity of billing and collecting.

In 1980, the late Arnold Relman, former editor of the *New England Journal of Medicine*, saw the handwriting on the wall of the business intrusion on patient care with his article, "The New Medical–Industrial Complex". Forty-two years later, Doctor Relman would not likely be surprised but on the other hand, might be actually astounded at the degree of control that the health care–industrial complex exerts over the delivery of health services. (I had the privilege of meeting this great man on a sojourn to Harvard in the 1990s.)

The widening disparity in health care is due to a disproportionate allocation of resources to its business aspect, such as administration, executive leadership, accounting, human resources, facilities management, procurement and supply chain, and information technology operations. This results in the commoditization of patients as mere consumers and providers, including nurses and doctors, being burdened with a greater workload while being paid less and relying more on lower-paid physician-extenders, such as physician assistants (PAs) and advanced practice nurses (APNs), for patient care.

Doctors Beasley, Roberts, and Goroll (2021)[10] trace the origin of the use of the term "providers" in health care to 1965 in Medicare legislation for designating entities receiving reimbursement for services that are provided. The term became extended to other members of the health services delivery system, such as primary care providers, and has naturally been adopted by health care business entities because, as Beasley and others point out, "provider" is part of the lexicon for commoditized services.

The term can therefore minimize the value that ensues from the input of the professionalism and customization that each patient-physician encounter demands. Then the use of the term "provider," at a minimum, confuses patients as to where the connection for their health and well-being falls. Is it with

---

10   Beasley, John W.; Roberts, Richard G.; Goroll, Allan H.: "Promoting Trust and Morale by Changing How the Word Provider is Used. Encouraging specificity and Transparency" —JAMA 325 (23): 2343-4, 2021.

a "branded" health care organization (hospital, clinic, etc.) or is it with their personal nurse or doctor? Some may agree that the commoditization of the healing arts by utilizing this term is a sinister attempt to shift the inherent trust in the patient-doctor relationship to an equivalent and interchangeability with the organization. This is where my experience in 2019 of leaving a health care organization and becoming one of the "disappeared" doctors, with no forwarding information for my patients, is the type of dehumanization typical of the business mentality.

# Chapter Six

## The Health Care Executive Pyramid

*"Nearly all men can stand adversity, but if you want to test a man's character, give him power."*

—Abraham Lincoln.

Try telling the above quote to any chairman of any clinical department in a medical school or hospital, and don't forget the c-suite executive vice presidents of any major hospital. Their forcefield of power deflects any acknowledgment of humility. Actually, it would trigger a reflexive spouting of the most outrageous BS to patronize or castigate, depending on how threatened they felt amid their baseline level of insecurity.

Some of these clinical chairmen, CEOs, deans, VPs, and others at the top of organizations have simply gone mad from the power they've been given, which has made any possibility of an intellectual discussion into a their way or the highway conversation. The authority of these tyrants stems from the control they have over money and the capability to appoint their cronies to positions of power. Patronage lives in medical institutions just as it does in the streets and sanitation department of your city. Don't ever be persuaded otherwise.

J. K. Galbraith (1906–2006), Harvard economics professor and presidential advisor, observed, "The salary of the chief executive officer (CEO) is not a market reward for achievement. It is frequently in the nature of a warm personal gesture by the individual to himself."[11]

One should not be fooled by the "not-for-profit" status of hospitals; their CEOs make lots of money. That status doesn't necessarily convey what it previously did in terms of an altruistic approach to providing patient care. Many such hospitals now make the most of this designation as a tax shelter, since the mission has become muddled by the emphasis on profit over patients.

This hierarchical arrangement of hospitals, health insurance companies, and other health care delivery organizations is arranged as a pyramid. The power of the pyramid as an organizational structure can be designed as either humanitarian (Maslow[12]) or business (health care–industrial complex). Arranged as a pyramid for business operations the focus is on profit. The determination of value in health care is challenging, at best, and contentious for those who actually work at the point of care. The salaries of CEOs of hospitals

---

11    Retrieved December 18, 2023 from BrainyQuote.com

12    Abraham Maslow (1908–1970), an anthropologist, developed a psychological theory in the mid-20th century to understand human motivation and behavior. It is typically depicted as a pyramid with five levels of needs arranged in a hierarchical order from the most basic physiological needs at the bottom to the highest level of self-actualization at the top.

and hospital systems, medical school deans, insurance executives, pharmacy benefit managers, etc., dictated by pyramidal hierarchies, extract value from patient care out of proportion to their administrative functions.

Who can blame them for feasting upon the compensation structure derived from business pyramids that form the hierarchy of health care organizations? It's always good to be king (i.e., CEO, chairman, dean, etc.).

As the gap between the salaries of those on the frontline of patient care and those of the executive suite grows, it mirrors the startling inequity between worker and management in other industries. Unfortunately, this inequity validates some of the observations of Karl Marx, who described the corrosive effects that "the control of the means of production" has on the worker. In health care, substitute the hospital for means of production for the "workers" in the specialties of transplants, cardiovascular surgery, and neurosurgery. John B. McKinlay and Joan Arches (1985) anticipated this class struggle and proletarianization[13] of physicians.

In Becker's Health Care online publication, Laura Dyrda, in an article titled, "Physician vs Healthcare CEO Pay: 5 notes," reported that the average physician salaries in 2021 ranged from $242,000 for primary care physicians to $511,000 for the highest-paid specialists while hospital CEO pay ranged from $274,000 to $30.4 million. The Health Care Delivery Management Pyramid bears little resemblance to the "hierarchy of needs" pyramid that Abraham Maslow formulated as the basis for motivation. Maslow identified, via his pyramid, ascending categories of needs that a person can achieve, starting with

---

13   Proletarianization in Marxism is the process whereby people move to being employed as wage labor by an employer.

the basic physiological needs progressing to safety needs to social needs to esteem needs until "self-actualization" is achieved. Self-actualization in health care delivery should equate with improving patient outcomes (equity).

Being at the top of the pyramid of health care organization, executives could not possibly be physically nor conceptually more removed from actual patient care where the true value of health care is created. Yet, the critically valuable work that produces the quality, safety, efficiency, and potential for cost saving at the frontline, i.e., the surplus value in Karl Marx's lingo, is captured by the health care executives' compensation. That patient care has become commoditized in the business model of health care is yet another reprehensible aspect of the influence of greed (Berwick[14]) on the healing arts.

While the nurses, physicians, laboratory technicians, housekeepers, et al, are in the trenches, the executives are principally engaged in buffing the general impressions of the health care organization brand and basking in the glory of the everyday miracles produced by the frontline, enjoying the reflected good deeds as a "halo effect."[15]

The "halo effect" is another form of self-congratulation by those who are at the top of a business organization, yet it contributes little to no material contribution to patient care.

---

14    Medical care quality leader Donald M. Berwick condemns the pervasive and crippling role of financial gain-seeking in US health care in an article titled, "Salve Lucrum: The Existential Threat of greed in US Health Care", *JAMA Network*, January 2023. "Salve Lucrum" is Latin for "Hail, Profit."

15    *The Halo Effect: ...and the Eight Other Business Delusions That Deceive Managers* is a book by Phil Rosenzweig that delves into the bias of the perception of the qualities of one thing being misappropriated onto other things undeservingly.

It consists of a group of delusions that produce the fantasy and false attribution about a business's performance.

The halo effect described by Rosenzweig plagues health care by virtue of a false narrative about where value actually occurs. To be crystal clear, it is with patient care and not fancy lobbies and art collections of hospitals. It certainly in no way, shape, or form resides with an executive many floors removed from a successful heart-lung transplantation operation, for example.

Unfortunately, the corrupt pyramid of the hierarchical organization of administration of hospitals, health insurance companies, and agencies obscures both the value-producing activities of patient care and reinforces its stranglehold on this effort through a series of blind spots.

This false narrative about health care organizations is reinforced by marketing and advertising budgets pouring money into their dubious pursuit instead of investing that money into transforming the quality, safety, and efficiency of patient care *(see Table One)*.

## Table One

### Blind Spots of Health Organization Hierarchies

- The power of the pyramid: Maslow (humanitarian; self-actualization, value producing throughout an organization) vs. "it's good to be King" (the model of the ancient Pharaohs).
- Domain knowledge vs. business school credentials (*From Higher Aims to Hired Hands*, Khurana, 2007).
- Character
  » Trust/loyalty/reciprocity.
  » Credibility (domain knowledge of patient health care).
  » Authenticity (when "true north" becomes a template).
  » Walking the talk ("The Invisible Man").
  » Talking the walk (BS, sophistry, groupthink).
- Power
  » Commoditization and the "myth" of control.
  » "Groupthink" — a term coined by William H. Whyte in his book *The Organization Man* (1956)..
- *The Emperor has No Clothes: The Halo Effect* (Rosenzweig), "survivorship bias," etc.
- Leadership "development."

- Hope is not a strategy.
- Risk aversion and deficit of ideas: focusing on the process over innovation (e.g., "car manufacturing" in the hernia clinic).

# Chapter Seven

## Why Ignoring the Coming Obsolescence of Hospitals is Holding Health Care Equality Back

In an article in *The Atlantic* magazine, July/August 2021, staff writer Kaitlyn Tiffany asked former Treasury Secretary Larry Summers about Eastman Kodak's future. His response about the once dominant leader in the photography world was, "Kodak is no longer an institution that is of great significance for the American economy." He said that "excessive nostalgia" had led to the company's downfall.

The article by the former Rochester, New York resident made a personal point: "I like listening to any Kodak story for a little bit at a time, to remind myself that I'm susceptible to 'excessive nostalgia,' which may be the same thing as what Joan Didion once called 'pernicious nostalgia.'"

When "pernicious nostalgia" takes over and clouds the ability to see change coming, then, Houston, we have a problem.

This nostalgia for the industries of old also applies to hospitals. Great, amazing, and wonderful things occur in hospitals.[16] In Ms. Tiffany's article, it was her fond memories of growing up in Rochester, NY—the home of Kodak—and its tale of collapse that evoked that excessive nostalgia. For me and other physicians and nurses of my era, it is the hospital of yesteryear over which we reminisce—a time when nurses and doctors called the shots (literally).

I can't escape my idealism regarding hospitals as temples of healing and observing heroic acts of courage of patients as they undergo treatment. However, my lingering idealism crashes into the reality that hospitals have become businesses that are just too big to manage safely and achieve high uniform standards of access, quality, and efficiency. How long can even those hospitals that have gone from "good to great"[17] be able to sustain the promise?

Hospitals, like any other organization, have both strengths and weaknesses. Despite this, frontline health care professionals such as nurses, doctors, pharmacists, and the rest of the care team remain committed to the principles of the healing arts and consistently exhibit exceptional dedication to helping their patients. However, the back office of administration and executive suites present a different reality. Although they may be business slanted, the understanding of what the flagship service of hospitals is has been lost. The administrative side of hospitals has become increasingly bloated in order to meet the demands imposed by government regulations and commercial health insurance. While the interaction between health care providers and patients is the critical component in creating value in patient care, a significant amount of their

---

16  I have seen and participated in them during over forty years in the OR.

17  Referencing Jim Collins' book of the same title; HarperCollins.

time is spent away from patients on tasks such as data entry via the electronic medical record. It is estimated that the actual patient–provider encounter, diagnosis, and treatment accounts for only about 20% of the patient care effort in a hospital.

Whether principally due to self-delusion or inertia, hospital executives will fiercely defend the transformation of hospital care delivery in its present mode. Despite having exhausted all the potential benefits of this model, they persist because they lack alternatives. These individuals in high-level positions in hospitals capture whatever "surplus income" that third-party payers pay for health care through the efforts of doctors and nurses.

In Marx's theory, "surplus value" refers to the amount of value that a worker produces above and beyond what they are paid for their labor. According to Marx, the surplus value created by workers is exploited. This behavior brings to mind a quote from a 19th-century British journalist, economist, and writer, best known for his influential works on economics and finance, Walter Bagehot, which goes as follows: "It is much easier to take other people's work and call it your own than it is to do your own work."

Is this part of the job description of the heads of hospitals or their counterparts in commercial health insurance companies? Aren't they deriving their salaries from the "surplus value" created by nurses and physicians, patient care activities, and through distortions to market processes like restriction of competition?

As stated in authors Brink Lindsey and Steven Teles' book, *The Captured Economy: How the Powerful Enrich Themselves, Slow Down Growth, and Increase Inequality*, "To the extent that rent-seeking holds sway, the invisible hand of capitalism degenerates into the grasping hand of crony capitalism." This observation highlights the difference within a system in which special interests use their influence to gain economic advantage at the expense of others. The authors argue that rent-seeking behavior, where individuals and firms seek to capture economic rents through political means, undermines the efficiency and fairness of the market system. The quote serves as a warning against such dangers and the need to maintain a level playing field for all participants in the market.

Along these lines, hospitals continue to expend their resources on barriers to entry and maintaining monopolies by influencing CON (certificate of need), state regulatory committees, to block free-standing ASCs (ambulatory surgery centers)—usually owned at least in part by surgeons. CON is a state-by-state political forum that decides whether a new health care facility may be built. It's a political process. Most existing health care facilities, i.e., hospitals, don't look kindly to the competition of their best surgeons opening an ASC on the next block. Competition is good, but not in their neighborhood.

A quote that is often attributed to Greg Scandlen[18] highlights the resistance that hospitals may have towards ASCs, which are medical facilities that perform same-day surgical procedures. According to Scandlen, hospitals may view the competition from ASCs, particularly when they are started by top surgeons from the hospital, as a threat to their own

---

18   Greg Scandlen is a health care policy analyst and advocate known for his work on health care reform and consumer-driven health care.

business. This highlights the tension that can exist between different health care providers in a competitive market and the challenges that ASCs can face in trying to establish themselves as viable alternatives to hospitals for surgical procedures.

ASCs are often less costly for patients compared to having the same procedure performed in a hospital. This is because ASCs have lower overhead costs than hospitals and are able to offer surgical procedures on an outpatient basis, which eliminates the need for an overnight stay in a hospital. Additionally, ASCs typically are more focused on a smaller range of services, which can also result in lower costs for patients. This raises the point once again about the possible conflict of interest for patient value versus hospital bottom lines.

While the hospital remains critical for supporting highly specialized care like neurosurgery and cardio-vascular (CV) surgery, the price that hospitals charge for the "facility fees" of these services includes significant management up-charging that adds thousands of dollars to the patient care. With the opaqueness of hospital pricing, determining the true cost of the famous "aspirin tablet for $100" remains a mystery. Recently, a law enacted in 2021 to require hospitals to post their prices has met with delay and blowback from hospitals' lobbying arm.

Will hospitals survive in a meaningful way? While hospital chains may appear as a typical market player, a closer examination reveals a lack of competition based on factors such as price, quality, and outcome. Due to this absence of competition, the health care industry works through dysfunctional markets.

Nobel Prize-winning economist and expert in game theory Thomas Schelling, in his book *Micromotives and Macrobehavior*, explores how individual behavior can lead to unintended and often undesirable outcomes at the societal level. In his quote, "Things don't work out optimally for a simple reason: there is no reason why they should." Schelling highlights the idea that social and economic systems don't necessarily work optimally because there is no inherent reason why they should. Schelling argues that individual actions, even when motivated by self-interest, can lead to collective outcomes that are far from optimal for society as a whole. The quote serves as a reminder of the complex and often unpredictable nature of social and economic systems and the need for careful analysis and understanding in order to produce desirable outcomes.

The dysfunctional markets created by the imposition of marketplace economics—not only on hospitals but all of the other ancillary components of patient care, i.e., finance, federal government programs of Medicare/Medicaid, Obamacare, and commercial health insurance, training of nurses, doctors, and allied medical specialists—creates the management apparatus necessary to deal with this complexity. All of these functions of administration and management are "free-riders" drafting the dedication of nurses, doctors, and other frontline health care providers.

Health insurance, by creating a reliance that shields individuals from the cost of care, contributes to the inefficiency of health care markets through the phenomenon of moral hazard.[19] This lessens individuals' personal accountability for their health and further exacerbates the dysfunctionality of the health care industry.

The trend that myself and my colleagues observed was that, as hospitals increased their power and market dominance through mergers and acquisitions, it led to a decrease in our ability to have a say in strategy or impact care decisions. Why can't "providers" own hospitals? The reason providers cannot own hospitals is that hospital systems wield their monopolistic economic or political power to suppress competition.

In the third-largest city in the United States, where I have practiced for over forty years, the alignment of numerous hospitals within a handful of corporations has suppressed opportunities for practicing my craft. The limited options were not based on abilities but rather on politics.

How do hospitals address their responsibility to meet rising demands for accessibility, quality, and safety? By employing a merger and acquisition strategy characterized by a defensive circling of the wagons, they acquire the competition of the few remaining standalone hospitals, thereby strengthening their monopoly power. This approach further separates chain hospitals from the communities that support them. In the Chicagoland area, for instance, there are now almost more hospital systems than standalone hospitals. The executive staff of these systems are often stationed remotely, receiving reports from local management teams.

Market dominance for hospital systems perpetuates their adherence to the conventional and unoriginal model of hospital strategy and operations. It has been hindering the

---

19  Moral hazard is a term used in economics and finance to describe a situation in which one party is able to take risks because it does not have to bear the full consequences of those risks. In other words, it occurs when individuals or entities can make decisions that involve risk-taking because they know they won't be responsible for all the potential negative outcomes.

emergence of innovation that could eventually replace the existing model by addressing the critical needs of inequality in the current system that has existed for over a century. Hospital consolidation fosters anticompetitive forces (Leemore Dafney 2021). In health care markets that are already dysfunctional to begin with due to uneven management structure, Dafney points out that focus on profit drives consolidation.

Hospitals, like coal-fired power plants and the environment, present significant compromises in terms of the value of the patient care services they provide. They should not be mistaken for centers of innovation; their executives always prioritize cost over value because they are trained on spreadsheets over patient care outcomes.

# Chapter Eight

# The Word Salad that Dominates Our Health Care

Beware the effect of cloaking of unintended consequences on your health by seemingly benign initials of government programs. In the end, as always, you get what you pay for one way or another—or as Milton Friedman said, "There is no free lunch."[20]

The US Congress has a reputation for naming complex legislation involving a lot of taxpayer money that comes to be referred to by initials. These pieces of legislation involving health care not only have a major impact on 20% of our economy (such as health care) but are rarely read by the politicians who pass them.

For example, the Health Insurance Portability and Accountability Act (HIPAA) of 1996 was enacted with the intention of safeguarding the security and confidentiality of medical information. Despite this aim, the frequent breaches of

---

20  Friedman's phrase implies that no government program is free. The taxpayer always pays an expensive bill in the end. He has won the Nobel Prize and advised President Regan, among other accolades.

electronic medical record (EMR) systems subsequently mandated by the Health Information Technology for Economic and Clinical Health Act of 2009 (HITECH) have produced significant compromises of the original intent of HIPAA. Nonetheless, the increased adoption and implementation of EMR systems has been a goldmine for those companies involved in their development despite their security flaws.

Another term for HIPAA in this context therefore might have been more appropriately the "Health Information (Industry) Profit Propagation Act." An unintended consequence of HIPAA was the collection of "big data" of patient health information, which has been spun off into yet other health care-related big business.

Similar "unintended" consequences have occurred with Obamacare, the so-called Patient Protection and Accountable Care Act (PPACA) of 2010. In this regard, the question for patients should be: how does this act protect them? For nurses and doctors, where does the accountability for care reside? Is it with those who are actually caring for the patient or with the "Payor Protection and Access (to) Care Association", aka the health insurance industry and its codependents—the hospitals? One thing is clear: profit is always protected.

The seemingly benign nature of the HIPAA and PPACA health care acts mask the significant influence of economic motives for businesses on the allocation of resources for patient care. Now enter, courtesy of the Covid-19 pandemic, another sop to hospitals and the health insurance industry. The CARES Act (Coronavirus Aid, Relief, and Economic Security) was introduced by the US Department of Health and Human Services on September 29, 2021: "HHS announces the availability of $25.5 billion in Covid-19 provider funding," which looks to be nothing more than corporate welfare.

Now, post-pandemic, in 2023, these hospitals are again drowning in red ink. This is due to the dependence of hospitals on maximizing income from procedures, such as orthopedic surgery, which have yet to be restored to full volume post-pandemic.

While the CARES Act temporarily forestalled the Covid-19 pandemic's financial meltdown of hospitals, their management must face these facts. Medicare, which pays for the majority of hip and knee replacements, provides more health care financing for the growing aging US population and is a loss-leader for inpatient hospital services.

Though it might be challenging to get a politician to admit that Medicare is obsolete as a viable economic program, empirical evidence speaks for itself. Its runaway utilization and costs far outstripping taxpayer revenue make it projected to run out of funding as soon as 2026. The original 1965 program enacted as a "pay as you go" system has long demonstrated its inefficiency and inability of its ever-growing bureaucracy to cope with demands almost 60 years later. All the tinkering with it that has transpired since 1964 is akin to rearranging the deck chairs on the Titanic. Nothing will change the inevitable collapse of Medicare (especially not Bernie Sanders' further socialization of the program). Medicare requires a complete overhaul not based upon political promises but on sound economic principles. Yet, politicians like Bernie want to include additional services of dental, vision, and hearing to it as the US "builds back better" from the Covid pandemic. Some feckless politicians tout making it "Medicare-for-all."

There is no argument here about providing care to those in need. But beyond urgent care outside of the alphabet programs, who pays? Nobel Prize-winning economist, the late Milton Friedman (1912–2006), observed that nothing is ever free. This totem of economics (trade-offs between unlimited demand and limited resources) runs right up against the politics that created Medicare/Medicaid and other alphabet acts of government health care.

Politicians, so limited on many fronts, always adopt a predictable fallback position when it comes to social programs. The National Health Service in Britain is facing the same type of political challenges. Medicare represents the continual challenge of legislative bodies to "do something" about a societal problem without any consideration for the long run. The aging population worldwide raises the specter of the collapse of health care.

Thomas Sowell, in his book *Applied Economics*, highlights the ongoing challenge faced by legislative bodies to address societal problems through legislation such as Medicare enacted in 1965. According to Sowell, such actions are often taken without sufficient consideration of their long-term consequences. Sowell's economics emphasizes the importance of considering the unintended consequences of government intervention in the economy and the need for a realistic evaluation of the costs and benefits of such policies. In the case of Medicare, Sowell's perspective suggests that the effects of the program on the health care system and the economy as a whole should be carefully evaluated over time to ensure that the original goals of the legislation are being met.

As such, from Sowell's economic perspective, the lack of economic analysis and consideration of long-term effects can lead to the challenges faced by programs like Medicare in the US and the National Health Service (NHS) in Britain.

This includes the depletion of funds in the case of Medicare and the inadequate provision of health care services by the NHS. Even before the pandemic, the failure to consider basic economic principles (such as moral hazard) and failure to think beyond immediate effects can result in negative consequences for these programs and the populations they serve.

Both Medicare and the National Health Service suffer from a lack of economic accountability in the provision of health care services. This occurs through moral hazard, in which patients and health care providers, insulated from the costs of medical care, encourage increased utilization without a corresponding improvement in quality, safety, and efficiency. Suggestions to improve the situation, such as asking patients to be more informed consumers and calling on health care providers to reduce costs, shift the responsibility away from administrators and the root cause of the problem. In fact, it triggers additional costs from third parties, whether they be the government or contracted commercial health insurance companies further accelerating the cost spiral. For example, offloading Medicare to Medicare Advantage programs has increased Medicare costs dramatically.

The HITECH Act of 2009, which was incentivized by the federal government for health care reform, was a result of the government's push for control over the health care system. This act, funded by several billion dollars, encouraged medical practitioners and providers to adopt electronic health records (EHRs) as a solution to the fragmentation in the health care system caused by the inability of doctors to communicate with each other. However, those who were subjected to the mandate found that EHRs were simply data entry exercises with little to no benefit and only served as a barrier to quality patient care. The HITECH Act is a prime example of the government's misguided attempts at health care reform.

The basic problems of all legislation by Congress to provide health care are attributable to either the blind spots leading the unintended consequences or the effects of influence peddling (lobbying) on producing programmatic expansion beyond the original intent. The lack of understanding of economics by politicians leads to the creation of large, unsustainable health care programs that eventually become too big to fail. This represents on their part ignorance, bias, or an over-inflated sense of self-importance. It is critical for politicians to take a more informed approach when dealing with complex economic issues, to ensure the long-term viability of the programs they create. However, mandating health services and then relying on the dysfunctional marketplace of the delivery system—a system in name only that features wide disparity of access, quality, safety, and outcomes—it is no wonder that inequality in all of those categories is the only constant.

Milton Friedman believed that after years of observing the federal government's actions, almost nothing positive could be accomplished by the government. While the United States Marine Corps and a few other noteworthy government agencies come to mind as exceptions, Friedman was not far off when it comes to the condition of Medicare, Medicaid, Obamacare, and so forth.

There is no solution forthcoming from those who use a fragmented approach to a fragmented industry. Recently, Senator Amy Klobucher, a failed presidential candidate in

2020 and noted "health care expert," has co-sponsored the "Health Misinformation Act of 2021" with Senator Ben Ray Luján. This will very likely dwarf my own efforts in the realm of health care reform and may ironically be referred to as the "Health MIA" if passed. Despite this, it remains unclear how politicians will impact the sustainability of health care.

## Chapter Nine

## Obamacare: Solving the Wrong Problem Precisely or The Law of Unintended Consequences

Some pundits could barely contain themselves as they trumpeted during the Covid-19 pandemic that the number of citizens with subsidized health insurance reached the highest level ever, and consequently the percentage of uninsured had dropped. Unfortunately, these individuals have blindly accepted the idea that having health insurance automatically equates to receiving adequate health care. However, those who are directly involved in providing medical services, rather than being ensconced in academic settings, know that commercial health insurance and Medicaid programs managed by commercial insurance companies may provide access to seeing a doctor, but there is no guarantee of the quality or timely delivery of actual health care services.

In that way, health insurance through "Obamacare" is much less than meets the eye. The Patient Protection and Affordable Care Act (PPACA) of 2010 is like any other government program suspect. For example, it contains numerous loopholes and exceptions that primarily benefit the wealthy business interests. Despite the history of the US Congress providing lavish entitlement programs, the PPACA of 2010 is one of the most ironic and misleading pieces of legislation in the name of health care expansion and reform.

The PPACA was minimally debated and crafted. According to a subsequent report by *The Wall Street Journal*, the 2,100-page bill was redrafted in an invitation-only, one-party meeting and passed by a razor-thin, one-party margin in a Christmas Eve 2009 vote, marking the first Christmas Eve vote since 1895. Despite being slimmed down to 906 pages, "Obamacare" offered neither protection nor affordable care. In fact, the act had no effect on malpractice lawsuits against medical professionals, therefore having no effect on higher costs for "defensive medicine." A more realistic name for this measure that significantly affects a large part of the US economy should have been the "Hospital Preservation and Health Insurance Company Subsidization Act."

Obamacare simply increases *access* to the world's most expensive and minimally accountable system of patient care—a system full of waste, fraud, and abuse with little practical means of recognizing the true value of safety, quality, and efficiency of patient care. Obamacare simply supplements the same old delivery process without creating meaningful incentives for innovation and reform.

By reinforcing the hospital and insurance company bureaucracies, Obamacare guarantees more of the same expensive and uneven quality of patient care. While a main selling point for Obamacare was that it would "bend the cost curve down," according to David Catron in *The American Spectator* in 2017, the subsequent doubling of health insurance premiums put this fantasy to rest. That fantasy refers to the idea that the implementation of Obamacare would lead to a reduction in the overall cost of health care. This was a key promise made by supporters of the act at the time of its passing. However, insurance premiums have doubled since its implementation. The reality of the situation may be more complicated, with various factors affecting the cost of health care and the implementation of Obamacare. Furthermore, hiding the additional subsidization of health insurance premiums in the CARES Act and other legislation does little to increase the value of quality patient care. While the total percentage of "insureds" has gone up, good luck accessing quality health care services with the Covid-depleted frontline nurses and doctors.

Obamacare's creation of "health insurance marketplaces" failed to provide adequate protection for patients and prevent medical debt, according to an article in *The Wall Street Journal*. The "failure to launch" of these marketplaces did nothing to improve health coverage and has left many individuals vulnerable to financial strain due to uncovered medical expenses.

In regard to actually reforming health care delivery, Obamacare created nebulous programs with platitudinous language so characteristic of the work of Congress and its health care policy consultants.

For example, such concepts mandated by Obamacare as "value-based payments" defy a meaningful definition of true value and elude the brightest economic minds. It's old wine in new bottles in the form of "the care delivery value chain." Schematics from the manufacturing company floor applied to headaches, cancer, and other ailments and diseases are mystifying. I'm referring to Michael Porter "redefining health care."[21] Despite Porter's success in strategy, his paradigm for reforming health care is a tough slog.

The problem of economists, with minimal domain knowledge in the professions of nursing or medicine who are involved with "redefining health care" such as Porter, is the assumption made starting with the basic definition of value as the formula of: "value = cost/quality." Although a fantastic equation for business, this is about as far removed as anyone can get from the unique nature of diagnosing and treating human disease.

Ludwig Wittgenstein (1889–1951), a philosopher known for his insights on the limitations of language, once said that philosophy is about freeing our minds from the spell of language. More specifically, "Philosophy is a battle against bewitchment of our intelligence by means of language." Wittgenstein's uncompromising stance cautions, for the uninitiated, that it might be best to steer clear of health care's complexities.

Paraphrasing Wittgenstein, an eccentric genius who did not tolerate fools gladly, it might be better for Professor Porter to get out of health care.

Channeling Wittgenstein further, economics applied to patient care misses the intangibles of empathy, communication, conveyance of relief, and other parts of a relationship in patient care that defies quantification and schemata. Access to lab tests and imaging still does not replace the quality of a health professional genuinely dedicated to the well-being of a person.

---

21  *Redefining Health Care: Creating Value-Based Competition on Results* by Michael E. Porter and Elizabeth Olmsted Teisberg.

Tragically, the Covid-19 pandemic not only took a significant toll on human lives but also worsened the already dire economic situation of the United States and the world. The health care reform efforts under Obamacare in 2010 were not up to mitigating these consequences. Subsequently, the American Rescue Plan Act of 2021, a $1.9 trillion economic stimulus bill, expanded Obamacare and resulted in an increase in health insurance premiums with no limit. This situation has been compounded by the recent passage of another infrastructure bill. Both bills drive up the cost inflation of health care.

## The Power of Fallacies

In economist Thomas Sowell's book *Economic Facts and Fallacies* (2011), he refers to programs like Obamacare as sharing, as with other social policy programs, the excuse that "it seemed like a good idea at the time."

One of the main flaws of the system is that it claims to preserve individual choice in obtaining health care by offering commercial health insurance or Medicaid enrollment. However, pre-Covid, as noted by Holman Jenkins,[22] the cost of health insurance for families without subsidies increased dramatically. This highlights the broader fallacy of the supposed "access to health care." Actually, most insurance programs have either high deductible costs or tight control over medical services.

Another major fallacy of Obamacare is that cost control of health care can be obtained by innovation to optimize value

---

22   Holman W. Jenkins, Jr. is a journalist and columnist for *The Wall Street Journal*. He has written extensively on a variety of topics, including economics, business, and health care.

of delivery, e.g., value-based purchasing and other deceptions of phraseology that a skeptical philosopher of language such as Ludwig Wittgenstein would immediately recognize as bogus wordplay.

Obamacare has faced criticism for its reliance on subsidizing commercial health insurance companies, which has removed accountability from these companies to provide adequate coverage. This has led to numerous accounts of inadequate coverage for medical treatment and price gouging by hospitals, as reported by *The Wall Street Journal* in a 2021 review on who pays the highest hospital prices. As a result, rising medical debt has become a reality for many people under Obamacare, with hospitals facing criticism for their debt collection practices (*WSJ*, December 27, 2020, "Hospitals Faulted on Medical-Debt Suits").

It's time to acknowledge the truth that the outdated systems of commercial health insurance from the World War II era and hospitals as the center of health care delivery are no longer serving the needs of the public in 2023. Merely surviving the test of time does not justify maintaining a flawed piece of legislation replete with unfulfilled promises and erroneous ideas. While at one time hospitals might have gone from "good to great," where are they headed today?

Tragically, the onset of the war in Ukraine (2022) has already moved the lessons of the Covid-19 pandemic off center stage as the specter of World War III looms. The war in Ukraine has led to a disruption of the world economy distinct from the worldwide bank collapse in the Great Financial Crisis of 2007–2008 and the 2020–2021 Covid pandemic crisis. With the recent surge in inflation in the United States and the ongoing uncertainty surrounding events in Ukraine, the interplay between the post-pandemic economic recovery and these developments is a unique and unpredictable challenge facing the world.

Amid the ongoing debate over Obamacare, there are those who celebrate its supposed increase in insured individuals during the pandemic, largely due to substantial subsidization, and those who have long criticized its unequal outcomes, driven by insurance companies' profit motives. However, there are also realists who recognize that, even with substantial Covid legislation subsidization, Obamacare still falls short of providing reliable health care for the majority of Americans.

On April 5, 2022, the White House celebrated the 12th anniversary of the signing of Obamacare into law, although the call for celebration may have been premature. Despite being in effect for 12 years, the issues or "glitches" with the legislation have yet to be fully addressed (as reported by *The Wall Street Journal* on April 6, 2022). At the April 5th ceremony, President Obama admitted that the legislation was intended to "plant a flag," yet some may view it as a surrender to the insurance companies and hospitals.

# Chapter Ten

# Health Care Economics Part 1: Survivorship Bias, a Scottish Professor, and the Visible Hand

*"It is not from the benevolence of the butcher, the brewer, or the baker that we expect our dinner, but from their regard to their own interests."*

—Adam Smith (1723–1790), The Wealth of Nations, 1776

The health system of the United States performs miracles daily as a reflection of the dedication and commitment to excellence by its nurses, doctors, and their allied health colleagues and teammates. As such, some consider this as evidence of the best health care on the planet, and in those situations, it is. What is not seen, however, are the failures of health care that occur in so many areas: high cost of care, uneven quality, delayed access, spotty efficiency, and not least, the waste that outmoded institutions and their organizational hierarchies perpetrate through inertia toward innovation. As with other large organizations, those on the frontline must always make up for the lack of support from the top of the pyramid.

The current perception of the effectiveness of the United States health care system is misguided and stems from the concept of survivor bias. There is an abundance of literature on successful hospitals; however, very little information is available on hospitals that have failed. This highlights the need for a more comprehensive examination of the health care system to understand its real strengths and weaknesses.

The human tendency to focus on success and overlook failure can lead to distorted perspectives and an incomplete understanding of reality. This is referred to as survivor bias, as outlined in the book, *Fooled by the Winners: How Survivor Bias Deceives Us* by David Lockwood. This book reveals the preference for happy endings and a lack of interest in reading about failures. This hinders our ability to learn from mistakes.

The story of Abraham Wald, a brilliant mathematician, serves as a poignant example of survivor bias. During World War II, Wald analyzed the bullet damage to allied planes (B17 bombers) that returned from missions over Germany. Based on the location of the damage, he postulated where to add additional armor to these planes. He realized that the planes that returned were only minimally damaged over the engines, the critical component aside from the wings for flight. Thus, he advised adding armor where the bullet holes were not, in order to protect the most vulnerable areas critical for survival. In other words, the planes that did not return likely had bullets in those locations, which brough them down.

Survival bias is a cognitive slant that occurs when individuals only consider the outcomes of those who have survived or succeeded while ignoring those who have failed or not survived. This can lead to an overestimation of the effectiveness of a particular strategy, decision, or product, as the negative outcomes are not taken into account. The focus on the positive results can also prevent individuals from learning from the failures or negative experiences of others, leading to poor decision-making or inefficient allocation of resources.

In the health care industry, the focus is solely placed on successful hospitals or systems as a result of a prevalence of survivor bias.

The overwhelming number of economists and commentators who gain recognition and credibility through their analysis of health care strategy and management, based on flawed survivor bias assumptions, do little to address the pressing issues of health care. As such, their combined effort barely makes a dent in solving the unsustainable path of health care, amounting to a fender bender in the parking lot of the local strip mall in terms of significance.

The actions of economists in health care can be compared to, as mentioned earlier, rearranging deck chairs on the Titanic. One economist, whom I had previously followed for his analysis of Medicare, may not have realized the enormity of the problem that Medicare has become, and how his efforts at finding solutions based on its 1965-era mandate, were limited as it drastically expanded over almost 60 years. Perhaps the philosopher Ludwig Wittgenstein would have told him to get out of health care altogether.

Such is the way when applying economic reasoning in the vacuum of academia or "think tanks" far removed from the frontline. The elastic demand for medical services crashing into the inelastic supply of health services is unsustainable.

There are many reasons for the fecklessness of these very distinguished experts. Principally, their futility stems from the embrace of the market theory applied to health care. For others, it is the hubris that comes from fame in other areas of economics.

Take for example the economist of note in one area of economics who has taken up health care economics late in his career to propose the "strategy that will save health care." Like a Texas cowboy who wrangles calves for a living deciding to take up alligator wrestling in Australia, one may find out the hard way that they are very different fields. As John Scandlen aptly observes, "There is something about health care that makes even sensible people lose their grip." Point well taken!

No one is immune from looking into the abyss of health care, such as an aging surgeon who takes up the mission of saving health care—guilty as charged!

The promotion of oversimplified ideas with the intention of improving health care through the use of the concept of "value" is misguided. Value, being a subjective term, can easily be misinterpreted and detracts from the crucial task of determining the real value of patient care at its core.

Economic models emphasizing maximizing value in patient care still rely on the archaic delivery system of past decades. If the production and consumption of health care follow any market principles, make no mistake that it is a dysfunctional market at best. The ever-escalating cost of health care does, however, follow some basic economic principles that can be identified as contributing to the inability of controlling its runaway trajectory.

Supply and demand of health services, like any other consumables such as shoes, food, etc., is all about tradeoffs and self-interest. The "invisible hand" of self-interest as the Scottish Father of Economics, Adam Smith, stated. The large administrative bodies of hospitals, health insurance companies, pharmacy benefit managers, and the Center for Medicare and Medicaid Services (CMS), operate the cost-controlling mechanisms in a manner that aligns with their budgeting practices, ensuring their continued viability as businesses. Providing people with the medical care they need follows a different agenda not based on profit and loss accounting.

The CMS, the federal government entity responsible for funding Medicare and Medicaid payments to hospitals and physicians, faces an annual budget projection and allocation for the cost of health care services, which amounts to billions of dollars. Despite numerous attempts to control the persistent rise in Medicare spending, the focus on limiting the cost has only been placed on providers, creating a situation in which their losses become the CMS's gain. This results in adverse incentives for the care of Medicare patients. When incentives, whether perverse or otherwise, exist in a system, it invites individuals who are motivated by self-interest, to engage in tactics that seek to manipulate or bypass attempts at control. Take Medicare again for example (Please! Take Medicare!). The Potter Report on April 7, 2022 reveals the windfall Medicare Advantage has become for commercial health insurers. Talk about self-interest!

In my specialty, treatment of a common condition in the elderly, lumbar spinal stenosis, treated for decades by simple lumbar laminectomy, now is combined more and more with a fusion that adds to surgeon reimbursement for the operation. That is due to the fact that where there is an incentive, sometimes the personal gain of the surgeon can obscure what is best for the patient.

For patients (or consumers), there is a self-interested incentive to obtain the health care they believe they require, regardless of the cost and the potential consequences of overuse—a phenomenon known as the "tragedy of the commons". The tragedy of the commons is an example of the self-interest of patients who have health care insurance of some form (Medicare, private commercial insurance, etc.) who tend to over-utilize it. This is a well-known entity in the insurance business called "moral hazard," through which there is a lack of incentive to guard against risk because one believes they are protected from its consequences.

For providers, the self-interest is maximizing income to pay off their investment in their education, expenses of practice, and taking care of their own families.

For health care business interests, it's all about the self-interest of profit, return on investment, etc.

We have only ourselves to blame for the current state of health care, as Scottish philosopher and economist Adam Smith theorized about this concept in his 1759 publication *The Theory of Moral Sentiments* and 1776 publication *The Wealth of Nations*. He posited that the aggregation of individual self-interest drives capitalism, as noted by Ryan Patrick Hanley in his book, *Our Great Purpose* (Princeton University Press, 2019) over the humanistic aspects of patient care.

All parties involved in health care, including patients, families, providers, government, and third-party payers are driven by self-interest. This holds true whether the health care system is market-based, like in the US, or government-directed, like in the UK's National Health Service. The pursuit of health care, like any other consumable, is driven by self-interest, especially when the true value of health services in terms of costs and expectations is hidden from the consumer, creating a moral hazard.

On more than one occasion I have had the discussion with the family of an elderly relative, whose condition was clinically irreversible, that conflicted with their wanting us to do everything possible. I explained with empathy that aggressive brain surgery would not bring Grandma back.

Self-interest puts untenable demands on increasing access to a health care delivery system that is unable to define value in quality, safety, and efficiency.

Where is the health care leadership to step up and speak the truth, to demonstrate the courage to connect with people who want an honest answer to questions about their health that is free from the self-interests of business?

Huge bureaucracies have developed to cope with the demands of self-interest leading to the pre-eminence of management as the mechanisms of tactics and strategy. One has to ask, how has management fared?

# The Cult of Management:
# False Gods and the Visible Hand

Management has grown into a significant component of any type of human endeavor. In *The Puritan Gift*, Kenneth and William Hopper outline its origins and development and how it has gone astray. Peter Drucker and Henry Mintzberg's career-long research defines management's entrenchment in various organizations across the world and the level of control it has gained.

Can the premise even approach reality that a business such as health care be fixed merely by managing it better? This effort has resulted in the creation of a class of thought leaders, academics, consultants, et al., who have become famous through books, presentations, and so forth, while lining their pockets as well. It's easy to offer observations, recommendations, etc. when you don't have "skin in the game." While the stories of these gurus make for interesting reading, the management and leadership feats of these sages remain one-off tales with little in the way of replication. For example, there is only one Mayo Clinic. Unfortunately, this effort has been effective in propagating post-graduate business education and the creation of cults that never really get at the heart of how we can manage to save health care. As with the enactment of Obamacare, the reality of the unsustainability of health care and meaningful reform keeps getting kicked further down the road, ignoring the failure to impact the basic deficit of inequality. I say again: access to health care does *not* guarantee that patients get equal access to quality, safety, or the best care.

At best, the management advice industry currently produces

entertaining stories and diversions as a form of self-help guides for executives. Hero worship and propagation of myths only contribute to the "too big to fail" crisis management of health care delivery today that blocks constructive approaches to reform of the same old practice that maintains a steady slate of inequality.

Fortunately, there are some who call it like it is and shine a light on the reality of these myths, fallacies, and delusions foisted upon health care executives who are desperate for advice. Henry Mintzberg, professor of management studies at McGill University, and Greg Scandlen, author of the book *Myth Busters*, present such an invaluable perspective of the effect of myths on leadership and reformed management in health care, and Matthew Stewart on the myths of management in general.

Mintzberg exposes the many fallacies of management plaguing health care. No sacred cow is spared as he shines a harsh light on the pet ideas of his fellow business school academics who have a lucrative side-business of writing books on fixing health care solely through business practices. As business school academics call for the "right" type of competition or competition based on value, etc. (Porter and Teisberg[23]), overlooked is the fact that business school curriculum is not part of medical training. These great women and men of academia (as the saying goes) are like the king wearing no clothes.

If the ideas of these gurus, such as competition, strategy, new definitions of value, Toyota Production System, etc., are so effective in fixing health care, then what has happened thus

---

23   Article: "Redefining Health Care: Creating Value-Based Competition on Results" by Michael E. Porter and Elizabeth O. Teisberg.

far? Where is the change? Where is the improvement they promise? The reality is that health care management and leadership have not changed their organization or process for decades. Sure, the titles may have changed or been added, like chief information or innovation officer for another six-figure salary, but the pyramidal organizational chart remains. Bottom line: more attention on business takes away more attention from care delivery.

Given the immense inertia that health care organizations store in their reverberating circuits of internal politics and intensive competition, it's no wonder that innovative leaders can possibly move the rock up the hill. If ever there were a hierarchy that was begging to be flattened, it's the archaic pyramids of health care delivery organizations. Actual patient care is about accountability. Whereas nurses and doctors are accountable to a relationship with a patient, the management hierarchy has no such commitment.

Enough observable evidence exists for one to logically say that the management hierarchies of health care delivery organizations are based on myths that perpetrate the waste and obstacles to producing value in terms of improved safety, quality, cost, and efficiency of patient care that only nurses and doctors can deliver.

Professor Mintzberg outlines myths perpetrated by delivery organization management involving "fads, fallacies, and foolishness" of administrative engineering, heroic leadership, and the right kind of competition, and perhaps the biggest doozy of a myth is that managing health care more like business will do the trick. Hello! Isn't the effect of the "businessification" of the healing arts over the past decades proof enough that "managing" to save health care is a fantasy?

Scandlen's *Myth Busters* book chronicles the futility of decades and decades of wrongheaded thoughts and actions that we have seen propagated in Obamacare.

Basically, as Mintzberg points out, "Being a business is bad for our health care."

According to *The Puritan Gift*, the "Golden Age of American Management" was the period between 1920 to 1970. However, since then, American businesses and industries have experienced a decline in the effectiveness of management practices, which has contributed to the financial crisis of 2007–2008 and the Great Recession. (That's the Great Recession of 2008–2009 before the next Great Recession of 2021.) Since the 1970s, the course of health care delivery organizations, principally hospitals, has followed suit (usually of the blue pin-stripe variety, pun intended) with more and more non-physician executives. And while the administration of patient care delivery has grown and continues to grow since the 1970s, there has been no corresponding growth in the number of physician executives. Consequently, innovation of patient care delivery is beholden to non-domain knowledge executives whose main body of work lies with the typical business functions of finance, supply chain, human resources, and other such areas.

As with the banking industry from 2007–2009, patient delivery encountered a major disruptive stress with the Covid pandemic, beginning in 2020, for which their management practices of health care, especially hospitals, were ill-equipped to handle. This was particularly evident as the sudden increase in demand for hospital support overwhelmed the supply of ventilators as well as the basic protective gear of masks, gowns, and gloves for the frontline staff.

This management failure had tragic consequences for nurses, doctors, and other health care workers. How does this happen? As Matthew Stewart stated, "Who manages the managers?" Or as the Romans said at the beginning of the end of their vast empire, "<u>Quis custodiet ipsos custodes?</u>" which translates to, "<u>Who will guard the guards themselves?</u>"

The stagnation of innovation of management in health care costs lives with the obstacles they erect through their ignorance, fear, or risk averseness.

Hospital managers find themselves in a challenging position between the leadership of their organization and the frontline medical staff. Some of them, who have previously worked as nurses or doctors, understand the demands and stress of patient care, but as managers, they are exposed to the distinct culture of business.

Now they are assessing the productivity of, perhaps at the least, their former colleagues or people with domain knowledge exceeding theirs. These are tough circumstances in which to maneuver. Yet the world of health care forges blithely on, even following the near-death experience during the Covid pandemic, when hospitals needed Congress to bail them out like the big banks of the 2008 financial crisis.

Will the culture of patient delivery organizations, principally hospitals following the pandemic, allow for a frank appraisal of their performance, or will its business culture simply close ranks and return to the status quo and business as usual while they stand in the shadows of unofficial PR campaigns that boast how well it's all going? Chris Argyris, an organizational psychologist at Harvard Business School, notes that failure can be a better teacher than success. Will executives of health care delivery organizations allow for self-appraisal to improve this situation? Or will the gurus and false prophets of the management self-help industry continue to overlook the fact that the emperors in the hospital executive suites who pay for their services are wearing no clothes?

Of the many, many books on management and health care I have read, only the 2005 compendium by Hoffman and Perry presents management mistakes in health care.[24] The lessons of the pandemic for hospital management and leadership worldwide are begging to be learned. Will the pandemic somehow shock them from their bonds of conventionality and groupthink in order to serve their patients and staff better? It is a solemn responsibility.

---

24  *Management Mistakes in Healthcare: Identification, Correction, and Prevention* Edited by Paul B. Hofmann and Frankie Perry; Cambridge University Press.

## Chapter Eleven

## Health Care Consultants: Eating the Brains of the Living?

In my view, Paul Krugman, the 2008 Nobel Prize-winning economist and primarily a latter-day columnist for *The New York Times*, embodies a return to the era when economics was referred to as "political economy." This discipline combines the relationship between societal politics, general policies, and economics and has roots dating back to the 17th and 18th centuries.

The United States health care system, which blends market economics with substantial government intervention through programs like Medicare and Obamacare, heavily dosed with politics and social policies, exemplifies the concept of political economy. Because of this, it continues to face ongoing challenges and deficiencies, creating as a side-effect persistent disparities in access, safety, quality, and cost of health care services.

Mr. Krugman is in particular one of the staunchest proponents of Obamacare, the federal government program to take over yet another substantial chunk of the US economy. Obamacare, similarly to Medicare, relies on the private health care network of hospitals, clinics, and physician practices to actually deliver health services to the American population. It funds these health services through a combination of tax revenues and fees. The commercial insurance companies, which serve as intermediaries but do not contribute to patient care, also profit from the system through the use of marketplaces, Medicaid management programs, and Medicare Advantage. Consequently, the increasing influence of commercial health insurance companies in reimbursement has led to their efforts in cost control through pre-approval scrutiny of medical tests and procedures. This has placed a strain on physicians, who are being pressured to increase productivity by seeing more patients. As a result, there is a growing divide between the management-focused third-party payers, concerned with cost control, and the physicians who deliver medical care. This conflict has fueled the growth of consulting in health care.

I share with Mr. Krugman the concept that there exist zombies or personages who can't see the forest for the trees, yet who hold out themselves as experts in forestry.[25] These zombies, by virtue of their indoctrination and/or education and training equating to brain-washing, arrive to fill in the gap between those on the frontline who "chop wood and carry water," in reference to Joshua Medcalf's book with the same title, and management and executives who lack domain knowledge of providing medical care.[26]

Separating the signal from the noise in something as complex as health care requires special ability. As the writer F. Scott

---

25   Paul Krugman's zombie concept is from his book, *Arguing with Zombies: Economics, Politics, and the Fight for a Better Future.*

26   Joshua Metcalf's full book title is: *Chop Wood Carry Water: How to Fall in Love with the Process of Becoming Great.*

Fitzgerald said, "The test of a first-rate intelligence is the ability to hold two opposed ideas in mind at the same time and still retain the ability to function." That's what makes health care so hard: reconciling the business operations part with the humanistic, emotionally intelligent part of the patient–nurse/doctor relationship, which is critical to acquiring the knowledge for diagnosis and treatment of medical conditions.

To help with this complexity, enter the consultants. Health care consultants represent a distinct category of enablers who feed on the insecurities and lack of domain knowledge of health care management. Consultants consist of two distinct groups: the professional consulting firms and the moon-lighting academics. The consulting firms are a story in themselves, having morphed from humble origins to cash-generating behemoths. Yet, the stories of those organizations that have gone down in flames with the clients they advised make interesting case study material for the academic business school consultants; for example, in the case of the Enron debacle. Consultants whose books, lectures, blogs, TED talks, etc., provide advice from 35,000 feet above the fray.

No matter which consultancy firm is involved, the process remains unchanged. Consultants visit the frontline workers, ingratiate themselves with their superiors, and generate a PowerPoint presentation or report that the frontline workers are expected to implement. This is a familiar scenario for anyone who has worked in the military or in a large organization, where such repetitive practices are common. American business theorist and professor emeritus at Harvard Business School Chris Argyris details this game in his book, *Flawed Advice and the Management Trap* (2000).

The actual modus operandi of health care consultants is rooted in a zombie-like model, in which they consume the knowledge of frontline workers and then repackage it in a form suitable for the executive offices. This repackaged knowledge is often presented in the language of consultants.

One of my favorite encounters along this line was a visit with the CEO of a local health care consultancy a few years back. I thought I was interviewing for a position with his group, but I soon realized this was not the case. The tipoff was his furious non-stop note-taking as he asked me question upon question about health care operations. I was filling in the blanks for him. No doubt, he was able to subsequently sell his boutique practice to one of the big boys and sponsor his own presentation at the hallowed local business school. Likely, I would have been better positioned to replace him than for him to ever acquire the gravitas to have credibility with the frontline that only can come from walking the walk. Yet he no doubt made a tidy sum with his consultancy.

One day, a good friend of mine and fellow care provider and I were discussing the apparent lack of knowledge by the middle managers and their consultants whom we encountered in the course of our clinical work. "You know, Dr. Cybulski," he said, "they were the frat boys and sorority girls out drinking beer while you were studying."

Another conversation with a fellow surgeon regarding health care administrators resulted in one of us saying, "You know we could do their jobs; they could never do ours."

Everyone needs to make a living, and the point is not to belittle anyone. However, the disconnect between business and medicine is fed by the belief that "business is a profession akin to medicine and law." It most assuredly is not. The daylight between the frontline of what nurses and doctors do and what administrators do is like that space between a Tiger Woods drive and that of an amateur playing partner—a space big enough to build a Super Walmart in. In over forty years in hospitals, I can count on one hand the times I have seen a hospital CEO in a clinical area, and that was when one was looking for his misplaced wallet. They just don't fit in, and they know it. Why is it that the least adept people who know the least about providing health care are running the show? The zombies have taken over!

What information the zombies of hospital management don't glean from the brains of the frontliners, they pay for with consultants. With so much need for understanding what they should do, why, oh why are they in charge? Who would better serve the doctors and nurses who are actually delivering that true value of services within the system?

The big business of health care consulting thrives because of the increasing complexity that business management creates for its own purpose and that ironically exceeds health care management's knowledge. Mintzberg aptly observed that "management thinking takes you only so far when the structures you have built are unmanageable." Why do they have the upper hand? Because health care is the financialization of the healing arts managed by business hierarchies that don't speak the language of patient care.

## Chapter Twelve

## We Have Met the Enemy, and They are Us!

Everyone who uses, provides, or pays for health services plays a role in patient care and thus has a responsibility for it. This includes all individuals and groups who are involved, directly or indirectly, in the delivery of health care. The only way to address the unequal access to quality health care is by acknowledging our shared responsibility and examining our own actions. Health care is a significant business in the United States, and the "selfish-interest" mentality of the zero-sum game[27] has unfortunately become ingrained in the system. However, it remains a moral obligation for health care professionals, particularly doctors, to prioritize the best treatment options for their patients.

"Tragedy of the commons" is a concept first introduced by Garrett Hardin in an influential 1968 paper in the journal

---

27  A zero-sum game describes a relationship, competition, or business dealing in which one's gain is the other's loss. The phrase "zero-sum game" has the notion that if one side wins and the other loses, this produces a net gain of zero.

*Science* that illustrates the conflict between individual self-interest and the common good in how resources can be destroyed or become unsustainable for everyone. Responsibility for stewardship of health care resources to distribute them equitably is an obligation of the highest accountability and obviously must transcend self-interest. The concept of limited resources, as demonstrated by this economic concept reminds us that we cannot overuse a shared limited resource to the detriment of others. Regrettably, this idea is widely neglected and even encouraged in consumer-driven societies, especially the United States. Unfortunately, doctors are no exception to this as they contribute to the estimated 20–30% waste of health care resources in the United States.

Nurses, doctors, first responders such as police and firefighters, teachers, and servicemen and women all share the noble goal of saving and improving life. However, as shepherds, we also bear the responsibility of educating the public about the realities and limitations of health care. Unfortunately, efforts in this regard might only warrant a "C-" grade at best.

While it is natural for moral hazard and self-interest to drive health care consumption, health care is not like a local buffet restaurant. Patients need support and guidance in making informed decisions about their health and lifestyles. Doctors, in particular, must be mindful of their own interests, both humanistic and economic, to help patients make the best choices for themselves and for their care. As health care providers, doctors must always advocate for their patients and strive to provide the safest, highest-quality care through unbiased diagnoses, recommendations, and treatments. Additionally, as doctors hold a special place in the healing arts, we are expected to uphold ethical standards that are commensurate with the privilege of our profession. These virtues separate the healing arts of medicine from the profit-driven motives of business.

Over the past few decades, the increasing industrialization of medicine has not preserved strategies for resisting the co-option of doctors' practices by business motives. A few years ago, I smiled upon seeing an article in *Harvard Business Review* that called for engaging doctors in the "health care revolution." Despite my search, I have yet to see signs of the promised "revolution" for doctors in the innovation of patient care. Meanwhile, more and more doctors are becoming part of corporate medicine or considering leaving the field entirely, which has been referred to as "Medicine's Great Resignation." According to a study by the AMA, one in five doctors plans to exit the field within two years. In 1982, Paul Starr's book, *The Social Transformation of American Medicine*, notes the successful establishment of "corporate medicine." At the time, I was too focused on my training as a neurosurgeon to be aware of these developments. However, "corporate medicine" overtook me and my colleagues in the early 2000s.

The reason for this is that doctors are our own worst enemies in the struggle to adapt to the shifting power dynamic in health care delivery. What was once a pyramid structure with doctors at the top, is now a network of businesses and government agencies that make up the health care–industrial complex, in which doctors are now in the majority akin to worker bees.

While doctors continue to play a major role in initiating diagnostic tests and treatment options, they are increasingly becoming a target for cost-cutting measures. This is particularly true in specialties that depend on expensive technology for patient care. Take, for example, diagnosis and treatment of degenerative changes in the spine. Degenerative changes in the spine, commonly associated with low back pain, have resulted in a multi-billion dollar industry offering injections, therapy, medication, and surgery. These treatments, many of which are recommended by providers with a vested interest, can be both costly and sometimes ineffective. This has led to the rise of the for-profit review businesses, which add to the cost of care but are necessary in order to prevent excessive use of questionable procedures.

However, the added pressure of increased oversight and review of their medical orders and recommendations can take a toll on doctors and their professional growth. Regrettably, some doctors may misinterpret this as an opportunity to bend ethical boundaries. I am not referring to extreme cases like Dr. Kervorkian, but rather, when doctors use their power to sway treatment recommendations for personal gain. These conflicts of interest undermine the trust between a patient and their doctor. It transforms the relationship from one based on advocacy and care to one driven by business and personal gain.

Many factors contribute to the limitations of physician adaptability, including other maladaptive behaviors, ranging from being socially awkward to being overly arrogant due to the power they hold over life and death. The ultra-competitive behavior that is encouraged in pre-medical students also has a negative impact on the ability of doctors to collaborate with others. Unfortunately, medical school, rather than addressing this issue, leaves students ill-prepared for the challenges they will face in the real world. This is the fault of petty bureaucrats and tyrants within medical school hierarchy.

However, there are exceptions, such as the dean of medicine whom I encountered in my first year of medical school in Urbana-Champaign, IL.

Medical schools, with the absolute power over the education of medical students and graduate medical education, are unfortunately often run by individuals who embody the traits described in "The No Asshole Rule."[28] With the exception of Dean Daniel K. Bloomfield, M.D. of the University of Illinois Medical School, many of the deans seen by the author were either ineffective, overconfident, or just plain jerks.

The politics of deans in medical schools can often be compared to the notoriously dysfunctional ruling practices of ancient Rome. Although physical assassinations are no longer practiced, the art of character assassination is still prevalent in academic medicine. Medical schools insinuate their control not only directly over their medical students and resident minions but also over the staff of the clinical departments of their affiliated teaching hospitals. That residents are a source of indentured relatively cheap labor for these hospitals adds to the power of medical school deans. Likewise, for the price of an academic title, fully trained doctors sell themselves to some of the most toxic individuals in all of medicine.

---

28   "The No Asshole Rule" is a concept popularized by Robert Sutton, a professor of management science and engineering at Stanford University, in his book, *The No Asshole Rule: Building a Civilized Workplace and Surviving One That Isn't*, published in 2007.

The central premise of the book is that workplaces should strive to create a more civil and respectful environment by not tolerating or hiring individuals who exhibit "asshole" behavior. Sutton argues that individuals who consistently engage in demeaning, disrespectful, or abusive behavior can have a detrimental effect on the workplace, leading to reduced morale, increased turnover, and decreased productivity.

The rivalry between academic clinical faculty and private practitioners at teaching hospitals creates a unique type of inter-medicine conflict known as Town vs. Gown. This competition does not enhance the cost-effectiveness, quality, or efficiency of patient care or the training of future doctors. The Town vs. Gown dynamic within clinical departments sets a negative example for residents, who often carry examples of this toxic behavior into their own practices after completing their training.

The stress of the medical profession has led to burnout for more than 40% of doctors. These stressors, which have been a part of the profession for a long time, can result in negative behavior and impact doctors' ability to participate in discussions around the delivery of patient care. The challenges to physician well-being can also hinder efforts to improve medical training and prevent the further commoditization of patient care by hospitals. This also impacts doctors participating in the critical socioeconomic policy discussions that affect delivery of patient care, organizing themselves in a manner to improve medicine's social armamentarium at the training level, or stemming the further commoditization of patient care as the strategy of hospitals and commercial health insurance among other for profit health care business entities *(e.g., the Aetna–CVS merger).*

The impact of business schools' practices, as outlined in *Higher Aims to Hired Hands* by Rakesh Khurana (2007) has led to a shift away from humanism as business trainees have taken over health care. Physicians, such as Zeke Emanuel, Don Berwick, John Toussaint, and Atul Gawande, have also taken on the role of consultants or thought leaders, offering their opinions on various topics related to health care delivery.

This has resulted in a cottage industry of "how-to" books and manuals that distract from addressing the real issues in the co-option of the doctor's role in patient care. Moreover, there are also "self-help" books aimed at insecure medical bureaucrats that highlight the tribal nature of health care conflicts and proposed solutions (Logan, et al.).

The obvious problem is that tribal behavior endemic to specialty groups is like lions that cohabit with sheep. Of course, lions couldn't care less about what sheep think. Medical schools also exploit their power over physicians, encouraging them to conform to academic norms. Many become assistant professors, associate professors, etc., and focus more on writing research papers instead of directly providing patient care. Deans take advantage of this by "loaning out" their clinical faculty to staff teaching hospitals at reduced rates, which benefits both the hospitals and the medical schools that co-brand themselves.

Let's be clear that academic titles do not guarantee clinical prowess. In fact, in many cases, it's the inverse. You don't necessarily want the professor or chairperson whose clinical effort is diverted by research and administrative efforts to operate on you or your loved ones. You likely want the assistant or associate professors who are performing the majority of clinical work for the department to be your surgeon. (This is one of the best-kept secrets of "prestigious" academic medical centers.)

SPOILER ALERT: For goodness sake, patients should be informed and be able to ask how often the prospective doctor is seeing patients with their diagnosis, operating on them, etc., and what their experience is and the results they have had. Rely on the various rating services for picking a restaurant and *not* your brain surgeon!

Unfortunately, doctors working in academic medical centers face not only the typical brutality of hospital politics but also the politics of the medical school and its leaders, requiring them to be subjected to bullying, political maneuvering, and compromising of their values.

When I first started in an academic medical center, a focus mainly on clinical excellence was usually sufficient. Any academic work, such as research, reports, and presentations was a bonus. Recognition and appreciation of this effort—that is, reciprocity by the hospital—was the norm. I'm not speaking here of perks and under-the-table payoffs, just an occasional smile and thanks from hospital executives. However, reciprocity faded as the era of hospital expansion has made the efforts of individual doctors seem less important, and doctors were folded into hospital-directed groups.

For example, for the first time since the AMA began surveying doctor's practices, in 2020–2021 more doctors were employed than had their own practices. Not only does this restrict the choice for patients, it also reflects a giving up of the fight by doctors against the medical–industrial complex.

What remains for nurses and doctors? The healing arts still possess control of the actual knowledge of disease processes, the ability to intervene, along with the opportunity for a direct relationship with patients. These are all critical factors in creating the true value of patient care that business models can't replicate. Whereas business functions of finance, HR, supply chain, etc., are ripe for replacement by artificial intelligence (AI), clinical decision-making and providing care still will remain in the province of actual nurses and doctors. The problem with the type of knowledge that nurses and doctors possess is that its power is more and more subverted by health care business interests.

# Transformation of Power

## Burnout and Commoditization of Providers: The Stoic Challenge for Resiliency

Admiral James Stockdale, the longest-serving POW of the Vietnam War, had obtained a master's degree in philosophy prior to being shot down over North Vietnam. As he was evacuating his crippled aircraft and parachuting into the heart of enemy country in 1965, he realized that his philosophical training was about to be supremely tested. During his eight years in captivity by the North Vietnamese, Admiral Stockdale underwent the most brutal torture, but his stoic philosophy stood him well.[29]

As an operating system for but in no way comparable to Admiral Stockdale's experience in captivity, the stoicism that he deployed is germane to a strategy for nurses, physicians and their teammates to work within the controlling and demoralizing tactics of the health care–industrial complex.

First, as Admiral Stockdale subsequently said about his strategy: recognize and accept the brutal facts of your reality. For nurses and physicians, the brutal fact is that, due to control of the means of production in hospitals, it is the management

---

29  James Stockdale's survival strategy revolved around facing the harsh realities of his situation squarely, without denying or sugarcoating them. He believed that it was essential to confront the brutal facts of his situation and uncertainty about his future. By doing so, he could maintain a realistic perspective on his circumstances and make rational decisions based on that understanding.
When he was released, he was asked how he made it through. He explained that the guards had full control over the prisoners' bodies, but the prisoners had control over their own minds. Most prisoners who faced the reality of their situation made it out alive.

class who are in charge. However, they are not in your clinic, at the bedside, or in the operating room with you.

The recognition of this reality has been occurring for decades, as in the paper "From the Doctors' Workshop to the Iron Cage? Evolving Models of Physician Control in US Health Systems" written by Martin Kitchener, Carol A. Caronna, and Stephen M. Shortell. This report and countless others explore the changing dynamics of physician control within the health care systems in the United States. And for this reason, the initial trickle of surgeons and their work moving to ambulatory surgery centers is now a torrent. However, compensation for value still remains out of the hands of nurses, doctors, and patients. As Thomas Sowell put it, "Why anyone would expect better decisions to be made by third parties who pay no price for being wrong is one of the mysteries of our time." Yet, this is exactly the setup by which the health care–industrial complex extracts value from patient care by nurses and doctors.

The other principle of stoicism, once you have accepted the brutal facts, is what you can control. For Admiral Stockdale, that was the belief that you will prevail in the end. The training of nurses, doctors, pharmacists, and their care teammates is demanding and harder than sitting on your bottom in a business school classroom, listening to lectures and case discussions.

Physicians always have the capacity to enhance the value of relationships with patients by offering empathy, in addition to medical knowledge that hospitals' financial transactional relationships can never provide no matter how much money is wasted on marketing campaigns and slogans.

Physicians and nurses, on account of their genuine credibility on the basis of their professional standing, play a critical role in trust-building and alleviating anxiety due to a variety of factors, including the misinformation that social media propagates as medical advice.

Admiral Stockdale would advise us to never forget this reality!

## Chapter Thirteen

# The Pandemic Disruption of Health Care

*"The very survival of the healing arts is on the line, and nothing less than a complete rebalancing of the health care system will suffice."*

—*Dr. George Cybulski*

The Covid-19 pandemic has irrevocably disrupted every aspect of health care and society in the United States and the world. This disruption will be felt forever, in every aspect of society and especially in providing health services. It remains to be seen if we can "Build Back Better." The early results are not encouraging. Specifically, regarding health care in the United States, the Covid-19 pandemic has burnt out the frontline staff—nurses, doctors, and their allied health support colleagues, and it looks like many of them are not coming back. While the "big box" hospitals have survived, rural hospitals, which pre-pandemic were already disappearing at an alarming rate, face existential threats.

Resident training or Graduate Medical Education (GME) was significant during the pandemic not only in terms of a decrease in hands-on experience of evaluating patients for residents but also by the adoption of remote educational conferences. What will be the response to this disruption? Given the reactionary character of the average medical school dean, I don't expect any significant innovation to compensate for the lost experiences for learning.

The effects of the Covid economic disaster on employment and inflation will continue to have secondary effects on the health insurance market, which was already dysfunctional pre-pandemic. Health insurance tied to employment will remain tenuous and subject to market forces that will be whipsawed by patients' post-Covid, pent-up demand.

Because the pandemic was so disruptive, it should make us reassess every aspect of health care in society and take this as an opportunity to redress the inequality of patient care. How can we provide health care for all who require it on a 24/7 basis? The prospects for this will demand entirely different approaches that will *not* come from those in charge before the pandemic.

For example, the front page of *The New York Times* on Sunday, January 16, 2022, reported on the shortage of nurses at Brooklyn Hospital caused by the third wave of Omicron. Burnout of nurses and doctors across the country is the legacy of the Covid pandemic in the United States. Very few pundits, politicians, and people seem to grasp the precarious position we find ourselves in today. That's because few health care executives have ever been on the frontline of delivering medicine and nursing.

Few health care executives have ever had the privilege and solemn responsibility of patient care. There is nothing more meaningful than shepherding the lives of thirty post-operative patients through the night. Few have taken a patient from the emergency department to the OR to save their life. Who's going to say what the value of these responsibilities truly is for the purpose of building health care back better?

Who can we turn to for answers? Perhaps Dr. Ezekiel Emanuel, a well-known public health expert, or Andy Slavitt, a former health care administrator, could provide insight. Or, as Colonel Jessup (Jack Nicholson) in the movie *A Few Good Men* asks, perhaps Lieutenant Weinberg could help us. I would hope that Mr. Salvitt and I share the same zeal for aiming to save health care but may have radically different approaches due to the fact that I have spent my career on the frontline and Andy has been a health care administrator.

Following the 2020–2022 Covid-19 pandemic, hospitals were kept afloat by the CARES Act of 2020 and are now standing in line for additional Congressional handouts. Barely surviving economically leaves little in the way for commitment to the mission of improving quality, safety, and efficiency. Even in the best of times, efforts in those critical objectives are often a sideshow that competes with marketing agendas. Health care is too critical to remain in the hands of system executives.

Health care being run by business minds is not working, and it must be rebalanced back into enhancing the value of the healing arts. This transformation will require an appeal to the better angels of mankind—empathy, altruism, and social progress focused on health, distant from the "repair shops" that predominate in medicine. A return to the spirit of idealism portrayed in the classics like Arrowsmith's "A

Fortunate Man" and others is necessary, and last but not least, individual personal responsibility for one's own health. The very survival of the healing arts is on the line, and nothing less than a complete rebalancing of the health care system will suffice.

Please read on to increase your awareness of the foibles of industrial health care and the potential for its salvation.

## Chapter Fourteen

# Trust Me, Everybody's Doing It! The Reality of Consumer-Driven Health Care

The infiltration of business interests in patient care has threatened to reduce the once strong bond of trust between patients and their health care providers to nothing more than a transaction. The influence of business-minded individuals and programs promoting consumer-based health care has only fueled the fire of consumerism in this field.

To be clear, this means that one's approach to their own health is now being treated as just another commodity to be bought and sold, like purchasing a car. Is this really the direction we want health care to take? If health care is indeed being treated like a commodity, then decisions concerning one's health involve similar considerations and risk assessments as any other financial transaction. This shift toward a market-based and behaviorally influenced approach to health care (consumerism) is aligned with the economic factors driving other transactions. However, while you can trade in or repair a malfunctioning car, you may have only one chance at repairing your body.

Health care, like car repair, is plagued by the issue of asymmetrical information. Asymmetrical information means that someone else has the power in a decision. For example, how do we know that the corner auto repair shop will fix your car correctly and not rip us off? Similarly, how do we know that all we need for a pinched nerve is a simple relief of pressure on a nerve root and not including an addon (upsell) of an expensive fusion of your spine added into the equation?

Fortunately, the medical education system and residency (specialty) training program required to practice medicine are rigorous and provide credentials to ensure a level of medical knowledge and capability. These credentials demonstrate a doctor's ability to acquire and retain knowledge. However, the transferability of this knowledge acquisition to effective communication, judgment, and problem-solving skills can vary greatly between doctors. Advancements in AI are expected to greatly aid in managing the increasing volume of medical knowledge to provide increased value for clinical decision-making. Nonetheless, asymmetry of information is the principal factor behind variability of outcomes in health care. It is the reason behind getting stuck with a "lemon" when buying a used car or picking a doctor.

George Akerlof is an economist who made observations about the problem of asymmetrical information in markets, using the example of buying used cars. He noted that in this scenario, the seller is aware of the true quality of the car being sold (e.g., whether or not it is a "lemon"), while the buyer, who lacks this information, must rely on averages in making their decision. Aklerlof's work highlights the challenge of making informed decisions in markets where information is not equally distributed between buyers and sellers. When a surgical operation is recommended, the patient takes all of the physical risks, but patient and surgeon should share the emotional risks.

Behavioral economics studies the risks and their role in decision-making. Professional liability insurance (often referred to as "malpractice insurance") provides a measure of risk management for the surgeon, and health insurance offers similar protection for the patient. However, both types of insurance have significant economic drawbacks.

For example, spine surgeons must pay substantial premiums for their liability insurance as a requirement for operating privileges at hospitals or surgicenters. This cost can potentially influence their decision-making and affect their recommendations, such as the use of implants in spine surgery (Eli Y Adashi, et al., 2022).[30]

Trust is a crucial factor in a successful patient–doctor relationship, but bias can obstruct this by clouding the determination of which side of the risk spectrum the patient falls.

As mentioned earlier, health insurance significantly impacts a patient's risks in terms of behavior. Moral hazard, as identified by economist Kenneth Arrow,[31] occurs when a person with insurance adjusts their behavior to take on more risk.

---

30   Eli Y. Adashi, Eli Y is an American academic physician-executive who, among other accolades, is Former Dean of the Division of Medicine and Biological Sciences at Brown University.

31   Kenneth Arrow was a Nobel Prize winner who made important contributions to the fields of welfare economics and general equilibrium theory. Arrow's work has had a lasting impact on economics and has been widely studied and cited. He is particularly well-known for his contributions to the understanding of risk and insurance, including the concept of moral hazard.

Unfortunately, health insurance does not provide protection against either physical or financial risks, such as the 19% of households affected by medical debt (Robertson, et al.)[32] Unfortunately, health care delivery systems have an outdated, reactionary approach to risk management.

---

32   Robertson, Christopher T.; Rukavina, Mark; Fuse Brown, Erin C.: "New State Consumer Protections Against Medical Debt" —*The Journal of the American Medical Association*, 327(2): 121–122, 2022

## Chapter Fifteen

# Health Care Transformation: Brutal Facts of Health Care's Pandemic "Creative Destruction" and Why Innovation of Patient Care is So Challenging

The Covid-19 pandemic was the "mother of all wake-up calls" for a comprehensive assessment of the state of health care. Apart from Operation Warp Speed and the development of a Covid vaccine, health care is in a precarious state. While numerous articles and books describing the failure of health care worldwide have been published, these well-intentioned works may ultimately be forgotten as the system's inertia resists change. The health care–industrial complex, while lending itself to frank diagnosis, is complex to treat. In fact, treating the maladies that put health care delivery in a pandemic near-death condition should leave no aspect of the United States' fragmented system unexplored. Let's run down the roster of the components of the system of health care delivery.

## Bureaucracy

The Covid-19 pandemic exposed the dysfunctioning management of delivery that has been heavily reliant on outdated bureaucracies. These bureaucracies are found in all aspects of the health care system, which include hospitals, health insurance companies, medical schools, academic medical centers, graduate medical education programs, and the Center for Medicare and Medicaid Services, among others. The bureaucracies of these critical delivery functions have remained largely unchanged for decades. During the pandemic, hospitals bordered on collapse.

## Health Insurance

The health care "reform" bill of this century, commonly known as "Obamacare," did not fundamentally change the entrenched bureaucracies in the health care system. Instead, it sought to improve the quality, safety, and efficiency of health care by creating mandates that these structures are unable to attain. Obamacare's "value-based" care initiatives seek to replace volume of care with value of care, yet value is in the eye of the beholder and not subject to ready definition.

## Markets and Value

The health care industry has produced a dysfunctional market for the delivery of health care. The actions of Congress, through its long-in-the-tooth Medicare/Medicaid programs (first enacted in 1965), rely for the most part on private hospitals and health insurance companies to provide the actual health services. Accountability in such an environment does nothing to meet the challenges of standardizing access to quality for safe and cost-effective health services besides strictly relying on the tender mercies of these corporations.

## Leadership

"The Hedgehog and the Fox," an essay by the philosopher Isaiah Berlin (1909–1997) in 1953, draws upon remnants of an observation by Archilochus, the ancient Greek poet who stated, "The fox knows many things, but the hedgehog knows one big thing." Berlin used this metaphor to distinguish the dichotomy between those who consider everything in terms of one perspective and those on the other hand who consider multiple, varied, and even contradictory ideas in their construction of an organizing principle and solutions.

Michael Ignatieff, biographer of Berlin *(Isaiah Berlin: A Life, London)*, notes this distinction between the hedgehog and the fox as a portrait of human dividedness. This division is apparent in the organizations that plague the delivery of patient care. Those on the frontlines who administer care must be flexible and know many things, and those in the back office who support delivery through supply chain, facilities management, finance, HR, etc. know only one thing—management.

While some of my physician colleagues might jump in to say that many hospital managers and leaders, due to their lubricious natures, are more like foxes, I refer to their decision-making, which sticks to a playbook of minimal risk to their authority.

This hedgehog dominance, which can also be known as groupthink, stymies consideration of the innumerable technological solutions for improving patient safety, quality, and efficiency of care. The disruption of the Covid-19 pandemic on hospital operations can either be looked upon as a double-edged sword—cutting away the dead tissue of ossified management groupthink, leading to a meaningful approach to innovation—or staunching the bleeding to preserve the status quo.

## Creative Destruction

Upton Sinclair of *The Jungle fame* (1906)—an exposé of the exploitation of meatpacking industry workers in 1900 Chicago—said, "It is difficult to get a man to understand something when his salary is dependent on his not understanding it." Some pundits estimate that health care is twenty-five to thirty years behind other industries in the utilization of innovation. The electronic medical record (EMR) as the primary source of technology for patient care is glorified data entry. EMR aside, clinics today look pretty much the same as they have for the past fifty years. While there are plenty of workflow-enhancing platforms available for patient care, approval for them can't get past the many levels of the health care bureaucracy where managers' predominant use of time is in meetings with "cost" navel-gazing.

Putting aside the tragedy caused by the failure of our government health bureaucracies, the Covid-19 pandemic should be a time of "creative destruction." This concept, defined by economist Joseph Schumpeter in 1942, refers to the process of innovative products and methods replacing outdated ones, ultimately causing the extinction of traditional ways of doing business.

The health care industry had been ripe for disruption for many, many years prior to the pandemic, but it has resisted attempts to innovate its core delivery platform. It is important to distinguish between the motivations driving the business of health care (profit with risk avoidance) and the motivation behind medical science (discovery of new ways to treat illness).

During the lockdown in the US, telehealth consultations saw a significant rise, but post-pandemic patient care is slowly reverting back to in-person evaluations.

In the operating room, advancements over the past forty years in technology have improved the lights and monitors, but as a surgeon, I still rely on the tried-and-true tools of training, experience, and insight to invade the body and address the source of illness. An electronic medical record is not critical to surgery, and it adds no value to the skills and experience required in the operating room. Even the widely-used surgical safety checklist introduced in 2007 has had no significant evolution and has become a formality. The actual "flight plan" for the operation remains firmly in my head, a "black box" if you will, based on commitment of all my learning and skill to the patient—just as it has been for the past thirty-five-plus years. This "flight plan" needs to become dynamic and shared with the whole operating team.

Certainly more robust safety measures exist,[33] but since it is not the administrator's neck on the line, and it costs money to implement, let's stick with the old one-page checklist mandate.

---

33   SafeStartMedical.com

# The Medical–Industrial Complex
## (Andrew "Bud" Relman, M.D.)

Capitalism exerts its dominant role in the United States health care industry. Arnold "Bud" Relman, M.D. (1923–2014), former editor of the *New England Journal of Medicine* (1977–1991), called it the "medical–industrial complex" in 1980, just as President Eisenhower coined the "military–industrial complex." And, like these other industries, health care has its own unique resistance to change, reinforced by entrenched beliefs and cognitive biases like the "halo effect" mentioned in Chapter Six. The halo effect gives health care administrators a false sense of accomplishment that is the actual work of the frontline heroes. The pandemic emphatically demonstrated where true value in health care delivery occurs.

Can we "manage" to save health care by management innovation?

The health care industry is rooted in outdated concepts, such as the Medicare program established in 1965 and World War II-era health insurance programs. Hospitals are stuck in the past, much like hotels were before the advent of home-sharing services disrupted the industry. The Medicare model is outdated for the demands that have been piled upon it, and the managed care concept has been reincarnated as Medicare "advantage" plans.

The health care industry is facing a shift toward an on-demand "new economy" model. While this new telehealth method of delivery offers convenience and accessibility, it is important to note that it is not a substitute for traditional, in-person medical procedures and surgeries, especially for complex procedures such as brain, spine, and cardiac surgery.

Hospital management will need to embrace innovation and move away from their current mindset, letting go of illusions and becoming adaptable and knowledgeable about artificial intelligence and technology platforms in order to continue improving patient care. Can Schumpeter's concept of "competition through innovation, whether of new products, new services, or new ways of doing business," gain a foothold in the post-Covid landscape of health care? It will require a strategic mindset disruption as well.

Such a perspective would be: use the convention of Professor James Carse in *Finite and Infinite Games, A Vision of Life as Play and Possibility* (1986); that is, life can be a finite game played for the purpose of winning or an infinite game played for the purpose of continuing to play.

Health care delivery as a business is a finite game played for the purpose of winning, and accordingly, management of it as practiced today stays between the lines. Creative destruction brought on by the disruption of the Covid-19 pandemic is an opportunity to create enhanced innovation for the infinite game of meeting the present and ever-evolving challenges of disease.

While taking care of the ill with the SARS-CoV-2 virus is very much about winning the battle for the patient and providing support for the frontline nurses and doctors, management requires commitment to innovation, which is the infinite game and where health care management critically needs to free itself from the bonds of outdated, reactionary risk management and bloated bureaucracies, and invest in innovation instead of padding the executive suite salaries.

Professor Carse's shift to an infinite mindset is critical for realizing "creative destruction" of health care from the Covid tragedy.

*The Wisdom of Failure*, outlined by authors Weinzimmer and McConoughey, focuses on the idea that embracing failure can lead to improved strategies and decision-making. The question remains, will the health care industry adopt this concept as a means of achieving significant improvements in patient care, or will it simply settle for maintaining the status quo?

As Dr. Relman did, I find much wanting in the state that the business of health care had devolved to even before the pandemic. Going back to pre-pandemic "business as usual," in which health care access, safety, quality, and cost were inequitable, is not the solution. We have to face the facts and responsibility for creating innovation for the infinite game of health care.

# Chapter Sixteen

# The Failure of Public Health and Federal Health Agency Administration

*"When we say getting back to normal, we mean something very different from what we're going through right now ... When we get back to normal, we will go back gradually to the point where we can function as a society (but) that might not ever happen in the sense that the threat is there."*

—Anthony Fauci, M.D. (From Brammer et al.)

It is not particularly reassuring to hear this from someone who purports to be one of the nation's leading experts on viruses, and therefore by extension the Covid-19 pandemic. Especially considering that they have spent over forty years working as the head of the National Institute of Allergy and Infectious Diseases. Dr. Fauci was surrounded by plenty of additional "experts" who rotated with him on the White House Coronavirus Task Force in both the Trump and Biden administrations. It has been challenging to keep up with the various recommendations for mitigating the spread of Covid-19 from this task force and other federal agencies.

For example, consider measures such as wearing masks. Was it double masks, not wearing masks, one mask, and so on? The one commonality of these "experts," by the way, which included professors of infectious disease, public health, epidemiology, virology, and more, is that mainly, their proclamations regarding Covid-19 have been consistently inconsistent.

There are a few reasons for this:

1. None of these experts have ever encountered a pandemic of this magnitude.

2. Viruses mutate, i.e., they are constantly changing as part of their strategy for survival and are correspondingly unpredictable "unknown unknowns."

3. The world's health care organizations aren't anything other than loosely affiliated political state, local, and federal bureaucratic arrangements strongly influenced by global, national, and local politics or business-driven delivery organizations.

4. While "experts" abound in health care, actual leaders are rare.

As a result, while it is easy to name the glory hounds, it is difficult to recognize those actual leaders in health care today. Sure, there are bureaucratic and hierarchical position-holders galore. In fact, the proliferation of hierarchy in health care management requires plenty of directors and fill-in-the-blank officers to report to those who report to those who report to the CEO, all of whom are indistinguishable but for their titles.

Add to this, many in health care who fashion themselves as "thought-leaders," those mercenaries who hawk their advice as speakers, management consultants, politicians, newspaper columnists, has-been economists, and so forth. However, just because they own a body doesn't make them experts on health policy or delivery.

The deficit of emotional intelligence among these "leaders" prevents them from demonstrating empathy, allowing unchecked egos and reluctance to acknowledge their own limitations. Hospital executives, in particular, often require the assistance of consultants, as they struggle to effectively streamline their organizations and maximize value, which can hinder their ability to effectively lead. Their failure to provide frontline staff, such as nurses, doctors, and respiratory therapists, with critical personal protection equipment (PPE) during the Covid-19 pandemic was a clear example of the supply chain breakdown, an indictment of feckless hospital leadership. What factors contributed to the inability to protect health care workers from this highly infectious disease? It is crucial to understand the underlying causes of this failure and to take proactive steps to prevent similar occurrences in the future. That takes accountable leadership.

At the end of the day, it was the frontline staff that was critical to patient care and who assumed the risk while the "experts" scrambled to come up with a meaningful strategy to mitigate the morbidity and mortality of the Covid-19 virus.

The striking difference again was between the professionalism of the frontline who possessed domain knowledge of patient care over bureaucrats and the back office executives who ran the health care–industrial complex machinery. Startling and reminiscent of leadership failure in the Great Financial Crisis of 2008 *(The Puritan Gift)*.

First, for meaningful progress to be made, it is essential for health care experts and leaders to acknowledge and take responsibility for their shortcomings highlighted by the Covid-19 pandemic. It is clear that the impact of the pandemic has been so significant that it will result in lasting changes to the health care landscape. We can only hope it is so. (*See Chapter Twenty-Two: "Lessons of the Pandemic: The Price of Panic".*)

In the book, *The Tyranny of Dead Ideas*,[34] author Matt Miller suggests that, as with other industries, there has been a continued reliance in health care on outdated approaches by experts in attempting to cope with the Covid-19 pandemic. Yet, like zombies, health care leaders march forward. In order to successfully revive the failing public health network in the United States, it will be necessary to move beyond the reliance on outdated measures and focus on innovative and long-term strategies that can address the failures that became so noticeable during the pandemic. As noted by "Zeke" Emanuel (2022),[35] it is clear that more fundamental changes are needed, and simply applying "band-aids" to a larger, systemic issue will not be sufficient. However, "band-aids" of reactionary legislation are what our federal government specializes in.

---

34  *The Tyranny of Dead Ideas: Letting Go of the Old Ways of Thinking to Unleash a New Prosperity* by Matt Miller. This book explores various economic and political ideas that Miller argues have become outdated and hinder progress in today's world. He suggests that these "dead ideas" should be reevaluated and replaced with new thinking in order to address the challenges of the modern era. The book delves into topics such as health care, education, taxes, and more, offering alternative perspectives on how to approach these issues.

35  Ezekiel J. Emanuel, MD, PhD, is an oncologist and world leader in health policy and bioethics. He is the son of Ben Emanuel, who was a patient of Doctor Cybulski.

Where will the leaders come from to demand accountability not for the purpose of recrimination but for the purpose of preventing other public health tragedies? Certainly not from bureaucracies steeped in failure.

# Chapter Seventeen

# It's Time for Health care "Leaders" To Take Their Medicine

*"One of the greatest reasons why so few people understand themselves is that most writers are always teaching men what they should be and hardly ever trouble their heads with telling them what they really are."*

—Bernard Mandeville, The Fable of the Bees 1714

*"We have to distrust each other. It is our only defense against betrayal."*

—Tennessee Williams

I've had a long-time misconception about the people running hospitals, chairing clinical departments, and serving as deans of medical schools. I assumed that they shared my idealism for the mission of patient care. Sadly for me, I realized too late that our approaches to patients were completely different. I trusted in my beliefs too much, and my disappointment was my own fault. It turns out that many of the individuals I encountered in health care were not nice human beings, and to borrow a phrase from Clementine Churchill's remark about a rival politician, "some of them are the direct descendants of Judas Iscariot."[36]

Turns out that impressive credentials, titles, and smooth talk usually mask a disquieting reality of the deception and manipulative tactics of some real jerks. As Machiavelli so aptly elucidated in his seminal work of politics, *The Prince* (1513),[37] these facets of human nature remain very much alive and, from my observation, very much in play within the range of medical institutions, including academic medical centers, hospitals, and medical schools. It is imperative that all who must deal with these health care organizations are aware of these Machiavellian practices and be equipped with the tools to navigate them successfully.

Power and control in the academic medicine landscape are intrinsically composed of the types of leaders who cultivate or pacify a herd of "excellent sheep," individuals who are blindly obedient to them and will do their bidding. Thus, *The Prince* is required reading as a survival guide of sorts for those seeking to make it within these treacherous environments

---

36    Judas Iscariot was a disciple and one of the original Twelve Apostles of Jesus Christ. Judas betrays Jesus by kissing him on the cheek as a means of pointing him out to be the one to arrest. The name Judas is commonly used synonymously with betrayal or treason.

37    Niccolò Machiavelli was an Italian diplomat, philosopher, and writer most famous for his work *The Prince*. In his book, he offers advice to rulers in positions of political power on how to maintain their rule. He famously wrote, "the ends justify the means," meaning that a ruler should be willing to do whatever is necessary to achieve and maintain power no matter how ruthless or unscrupulous it might be.

of industrial health care. For those who hold esteemed titles within the medical industry—the designations of chief executive officer, president, chairman, etc.—should be at least a warning and indication of caution. What it typically takes to get to the top of these pyramids—self-importance and a thirst for power—are qualities not consistent with empathic leadership. This is not to say that all top executives are this way, but the majority certainly are.

However, it is difficult to imagine anyone turning down a position that offers such abundant rewards while providing insulation from risks and accountability through shields of multiple layers of bureaucracy. In hospitals, the CEO is answerable only to the board of directors, which are frequently comprised of individuals who are either personal acquaintances, business associates, or golfing buddies of the CEO. Regrettably, these board members, while they may be corporate titans, are often ill-informed regarding the intricacies of health care. Knowledge of efficiency and cost-effectiveness, while great for running a beer brewery, does not translate very well into patient care.

In addition, board members of hospitals are fully dependent on the hospital CEO to filter and translate information for them, and usually accordingly serve as a rubber stamp for the CEO. Deans of medical schools, living in the ivory towers of the arcane world of academia, have even less wherewithal to recognize what quality of patient care encompasses.

In the United States today, the vast majority of health care organizations (HCOs) are run by business school-educated individuals with little domain knowledge of the actual process of patient care. While patient care involves customized processes not easily replicated by business systems, it doesn't stop business majors and CEOs from forcing the issue of standardization upon care providers.

Most of the workday for hospital managers and executives is taken up by meetings about surgical procedures, labor and delivery, emergency rooms, etc.—areas whose intricacies they barely understand. Administrators do oversee the critical procurement of essential supplies and medications crucial to patient care but can easily get lost in the weeds of details focused on cost over nurses' and doctors' dedication to what is best for patient care.

How much value do the health care bureaucracies and administrators bring to the table? Let's take the operating room table for example. Who should control the processes and material that goes into an operation? The responsibility of decision-making regarding treatment resides with doctors and nurses. However, the interposition of the medical–industrial complex adds business and political considerations to the mix. As a surgeon, am I able to use the optimal suture, implants, etc. for what I have learned to provide the best outcome for my patient?

Value in health care defies standardization. Consider the notion of "quality" health services. To a patient, the term quality encompasses numerous factors, such as safety, timely care, outcome, and attention to their physical and emotional well-being, comprising the overall experience of their care. For nurses and doctors, it is the patient's outcome and the ability to get their patient what the care they need in a safe, efficient manner. More and more, "quality" for nurses and doctors is being based on the ratings received from surveys dependent on factors beyond their control and involving perception vs. reality. The same goes for rating hospitals.

The Centers for Medicare and Medicaid Services (CMS) have implemented a program known as the "Overall Hospital Quality Star Ratings Program." This program, which has been in place since 2016, evaluates sixty-four measures in hospitals, including straightforward factors such as mortality and readmission rates. However, it also assesses more nuanced measures such as the "safety of care, effectiveness of care, and timeliness of care," which are highly subject to interpretation and dependent on multiple factors.

The "Star Rating System" for hospitals has become a significant focus in the hospital industry because of its marketing potential and connection to reimbursement. The cost of attention to doing well on the "Star Rating" program is dedicating personnel who otherwise could contribute directly to patient care.

Of greater significance (with a note of sarcasm), is the hospital rating system by the US News and World Report (USNWR). Even though its relevance is questionable as to whether anyone reads USNWR in health care today, a high rating is sought by hospital executives probably because their bonuses depend on a good USNWR rating!

The incentives and investment in care are diverted by these and other measures such as art collections and marble atria, which, to be frank, have little to no impact on the quality of patient care provided.

The divide between the bourgeoisie of hospital management and the increasing proletarianization of the frontline health care workers creates an atmosphere of suspicion. While my pre-med peers and I were riveted to study carrels in the Biology Library, our future health care management colleagues were enjoying cold ones on fraternity/sorority row or in off-campus watering holes.

Little did I know when I began my career in neurosurgery that approximately ten years later, administrators would have such an advantage over me and my peers. It wasn't until I became familiar with MacEachern's sellout of his peers (Chapter Four) that I realized how management had taken over health care. As Roy Porter noted in his book *The Greatest Benefit to Mankind* (1997), this takeover had been occurring while doctors were too occupied with patient care.

As administrators and executives have seized the controls metaphorically of hospitals, an alarm is saying, "Too low, pull up."

During the pandemic, hospital management almost took us all down with them. If it weren't for the arrogance of hospital CEOs and the barriers they erect to innovation and improvements, a person might actually feel sorry for these befuddled health care professionals. However, due to the excessive financial gains they make and the significant amount of resources they divert away from investments that could enhance the value of patient care, it is difficult to feel sympathy for them.

Hospital executives' blind spots, as illustrated in "Table One" of Chapter Six, mirror the flawed management styles of financial executives during the 2008–2010 crisis. As in the finance industry, a fatal management deficit called "cult knowledge" (MBAs) occurs in hospital executives as well. This term defines the insularity of business-focused people who manage health care organizations. The faults lie in the difference between knowing what needs to be done and knowing how to do it.

Decision-making for plotting health care strategy lies with executives, the majority of whom have a predominant business training and focus. Power for decisions affecting the way health services are provided paradoxically resides with business people and politicians who "consult" those from the frontline.

Health care executives, whether because of their lack of actual knowledge about true value and quality or their love of power, stifle strategy for innovation.

The cure for the fecklessness of hospital management? It's the "medicine" literally from nurses, doctors, and other humanists who see the innovation daily from the frontline.

# Chapter Eighteen

# The "Invisible Hand" and the Dysfunctional Market of Health Care

*"Nature's action is complex: and nothing is gained in the long run by pretending it is simple and trying to describe it in a series of elementary propositions."*

—Alfred Marshall, Father of Economics

*"Politicians, while of the mindset to do something, pay no price for being wrong."*

—Thomas Sowell, Economist

It has been said that caring for the sick is an art to which science is applied. In order to provide for the technology, labor, and physical setting required for patient care, management of the capital necessary to provide these resources must follow the basic law of economics, which is managing the demand for limited resources. Now, when demand for limited health care resources becomes unlimited, "Houston, we have a problem."

Economics, which is used to predict demand and utilization of resources, cannot deny the limitations of scarcity.

Many either aspire to live forever or don't give it a thought; others, when faced with the reality of a life-limiting illness, want to have everything medically possible done for themselves or their loved ones. Rare is the person who is able to face the reality of medicine's limitations in the face of their own mortality.

However, when it comes to health care in the United States, the "more is always better" rule applies. This demand is fueled by the actions of politicians who persist in continuously promising more health care services such as dental, vision, hearing aids, etc. in order to "buy" votes.

Politicians just can't say no to the limitless demands of their constituents (Sowell). To pay for these promises, a public-private financial apparatus has formed, commonly known as "third parties," which also can't say no to making money. By their role in the financing of health care services, these businesses wield significant power and influence over the patient-provider relationship, usually exceeding or at least monitoring the activities of doctors, nurse practitioners, pharmacists, and other health care providers.

Therefore, decision-making for patient care is subject to either political or financial consideration, or both, in terms of influence on the doctor–patient relationship. Due to the profit motive, return on investment factors into this relationship.

In 2023, United States health care expenditures amounted to approximately $4 trillion. In 2021, administrative and financial operations accounted for an estimated 15–25% of the total health care spending, equivalent to roughly $600 billion to $1 trillion. (Sources: Tollen, Health Affairs Blog, 2021: Chernew and Mintz, JAMA 2021)

That's right, up to 25% of health care spending did not provide one blood test or CT scan.

That great sucking sound is the siphoning away of dollars to those who barely know how to put on a band-aid. "It is not from the benevolence of the butcher, the brewer, or the baker that we expect our dinner but from their regard to their own self-interest" (Adam Smith, *The Wealth of Nations*, 1776). In modern times, patient care more is more dependent than ever on the benevolence of doctors and nurses who must compete with business.

Adam Smith, the "father" of economics, described the role of "self-interest" or the "invisible hand" behind the distribution of goods and services that create markets. When the "invisible hand" is balanced, all is well. However, market dynamics driven by the "invisible hand" of self-interest don't work very well for producing balance in the supply and demand of health care.

Benevolence stemming from the desire to help our fellow humans is the driving force at heart for those who become nurses, doctors, pharmacists, physician assistants, respiratory therapists, and all others in the healing arts.

The innate rewards of satisfaction when helping those in need must be balanced with the possibility of excessive self-interest as displayed in the doctor's parking lot filled with Porsches, Mercedes, Aston-Martians, Ferraris, etc. Therefore, self-interest can be a double-edged sword. When it's fueled by a sense of entitlement or driven by competitive forces, benevolence is compromised.

The "invisible hand" of self-interest among patients has been described in economics with the terms "tragedy of the commons" and "moral hazard."

The concept of the "tragedy of the commons", as discussed in Chapter Twelve, describes a situation in which individuals or groups share a finite resource of space, setting up the potential for competition. This concept has its roots in the historical practice of livestock herders, who depended on a limited grazing space known as the "commons" to graze their flocks in order to provide for their families. When an individual herder increased the size of their herd and thus their use of the commons, it was to the detriment of the other herders who shared the same space. This represents Economics 101 in which supply, "the commons," is finite while demand is potentially unlimited. This limitation, especially when it comes to availability of health care services has become obscured by the ubiquity of the profit motive literally putting MRI scanners and/or "docs-in-a-box" on every other street.

The insurance industry has introduced another principle that encourages increased self-interest know as "moral hazard." In the case of health care insurance, when third parties such as commercial health insurance companies or federal programs like Medicare cover the majority of health care costs, insulation from the cost of services unlocks demand. The Affordable Care Act (Obamacare) is a striking example of how moral hazard subsidized under the ruse of a health care "marketplace" stokes both demand and the health insurance companys' profit.

Moral hazard reinforces the consumption of health self-services by obscuring the full costs of health care. This can lead to an increase in demand for health care services and a corresponding rise in health care costs, as the consumer is less aware of the financial implications of their health care decisions. Increasing demand for a service of limited supply ignores basic economics.

However, as long as politicians and industrialized medicine support the myth that supply of health care is unlimited, then improvement of access to average or mediocre care will not be improved. When government and corporations dictate decision-making for medical care, taking it out of the hands of doctors and nurses, progress is unlikely. It is crucial to remember that medical care and health care are not interchangeable terms, as pointed out by Thomas Sowell.

Health care is a business that is primarily driven by profit, and its corporate-governmental process commands "the towering heights" (Lenin) of power.

## Dysfunctional Health Care Markets

The "efficient market hypothesis," which explains the phenomenon of efficient security markets that reflect all available information, earned Professor Eugene Fama a Nobel Prize in Economics in 2013. However, when comparing this concept to the health care market, it is clear that the health care market is dysfunctional and inefficient—a market in name only. This inefficiency is due to the asymmetry of information between patients and providers, which affects the optimality of treatment choices for creating value. Additionally, there is a lack of price transparency between providers, such as hospitals and clinics, and third-party payers such as Medicare and commercial health insurance companies. This dysfunction diverts resources to administrative functions and exorbitant executive pay. It's no wonder that the return on $4 trillion invested in this market has not been matched by corresponding improvements in access to quality health care for all individuals. Just the opposite, a startling inequity in access to safe, efficient care, is the norm.

## Consumer-Driven Health Care

It is highly unlikely that the concept of consumer-driven health care will be widely adopted until the day when AI-powered autonomous vehicles operate without killing pedestrians or the day when pigs fly. Comparing health care to diagnosing problems with your car's performance, just because you are able to drive a car doesn't automatically make you an expert in auto mechanics. Similarly, just because you have a body, doesn't mean you have the necessary medical expertise to make informed health care decisions. Despite this, there is a growing trend of promoting consumer-driven health care approaches as a solution for improving quality and reducing costs through various mediums such as books, presentations, and of course the internet.

I have recently observed that most of the time now, after my introduction and open-ended question as to how I might help, many patients provide me with their own diagnosis. Once I kindly explain to them that diagnosis of their condition is why they have come to see me, I begin the fact-gathering and enlisting their feedback by creating an open-ended, give-and-take conversation. As with a mother and their children and a pet owner and their pet, providing the opportunity for people to speak about themselves and explain the problem that brought them in, in their own words, usually allows them to reveal key information. Hence, the art of listening remains extremely valuable (though not likely to be recognized as such).

That is why pecking on the keyboard of the EMR is such a distraction to the patient–physician/nurse relationship, both in terms of taking away from interpersonal communication and relegating questions to a standard template.

The secret of caring for the patient is caring (Peabody) or at least looking at them.

In the future, medical diagnosis will be accomplished using AI as a cost-saving measure to eliminate the physician, similar to how a vehicle's software can diagnose its dysfunction. However, automotive technicians are not the most caring types. Therefore, until artificial intelligence (AI) can ask customized questions based on a patient's specific health problems, empathy and communication will continue to be essential to creating the milieu for obtaining information.

More and more, selecting a health care provider occurs through apps and surveys, similar to how one might choose a restaurant. Unfortunately, reviews and surveys aimed at assessing the quality of a physician are often unreliable and misinformed. Patients can harbor biases and agendas that are unrelated to the medical care provided, and these may skew their ratings and comments. It is not uncommon for patients to take out their frustrations about factors outside of a doctor's control, such as wait time or hospital bureaucracy, on the physician's review.

The reality is that finding an app that offers a comprehensive measure of a health care professional's competency, quality of care, and level of empathy is not as simple as choosing a car or a cleaning service. The intangibles of health care, such as bedside manner and communication skills, are more difficult to quantify and measure objectively

For example, selecting the right spine surgeon is a critical decision that can change your life. However, it can be challenging due to the asymmetry of information surrounding the expertise and quality of different surgeons, along with their biases based on training, experience, and self-interest.

In an attempt to provide more options and encourage competition, many internet-based medical options have emerged. This has invited into patient care the even less humane and more greedy private equity types. These individuals are unable to see the forest for the trees; money as the great motivator obscures any perception of the true value of patient care. However, the emphasis on choice has led to increased redundancy, which is a major contributor to the waste and dysfunction in health care markets. The appearance of choice often serves as a proxy for true value, promoting the false narrative that more options equate to better outcomes. Furthermore, this emphasis on choice feeds the illusion that consumer-driven health care promotes beneficial competition. As we'll see in the next chapter, the delusions are not limited to consumer-facing options. Unfortunately, many false perceptions also exist at the level of health care management.

## Chapter Nineteen

## Dominant Forces in Health Care Management: The Halo Effect

"What defines a good leader?" asks the character Sarah in James Stejskal's Special Forces thriller *A Question of Time* (2020). Sergeant Becker replies, "First, either someone is a leader or he's not. There is no such thing as a bad leader. If [they] are bad, [they] are not a leader."

Barack Obama was notable for exceptional rhetorical skills that helped sell himself, first as a one-term US Senator and then as a president. As president, he sold the people of the United States a huge expansion of government control of health care (remember his famous sales pitch for Obamacare: "If you like your health care plan, you can keep your health care plan." *USA Today*, 2013). In reality, Obamacare, billed as reform of health care significantly benefited the bottom lines of hospitals and health insurance companies. It continues to do so today without any appreciable improvement of the inequity of health care.

With this achievement, President Obama, amongst his additional accomplishments, such as the Nobel Peace Prize, etc., would seem to qualify as a leader. However, leadership is not salesmanship—at least it's not *only* salesmanship—and if he had architects and supporters of Obamacare think that health insurance equates to patient care, then fundamentally they are under a misapprehension of the complex nature of health care delivery.

All health insurance as a government program like Medicaid/Medicare does is get you in the door, sometimes.

After that, who knows about the quality of patient care services? Who determines the level of this always meaningful and sometimes critical care?

There is a common misconception that those holding high-ranking positions within government, hospitals, medical schools, or health care companies (commercial health insurance firms) automatically qualify as health care leaders. With rare exception, this belief could not be further from the truth.

In reality, true health care leadership encompasses a diverse range of qualities, skills, and attributes that do not come with job titles and organizational hierarchies.

Distinguishing those true leaders from those occupying a top position within an organization involves a commitment to ignoring the groupthink that plagues most organizations and how leaders are picked. Unfortunately, the proliferation of hierarchies within hospitals, medical schools, and health care businesses has resulted in a greater number of positions than there are individuals truly qualified in leadership to fill them. As such, merely occupying the top spot does not automatically confer leadership qualities, nor does it guarantee fulfillment of other traits necessary for leadership.

In fact, it is rare for actual leaders within an organization to reach the top position. Over my four decades of experience working in hospitals and hospital systems, I have observed that few individuals occupying leadership positions actually demonstrate behaviors that truly embody behavior worthy of being called leaders. Probably being called politicians or BSers is a more apt name.

The main reason for this is that health care is a business. Perhaps those who rise to or are appointed to leadership positions of health care organizations begin their journeys with admirable intentions, but the process of ascending to the top of business hierarchies is fraught with obstacles that often lead to the attrition of virtues and ideals. The journey to the top is littered with those who have fallen away, unable to surmount the political barriers.

The individual is the product of power, as suggested by the French postmodernist, Michael Foucault.

Years ago, professionals of the healing arts of nursing and medicine were in charge of patient care. While not immune to the human foibles of power and ego, patient care itself wasn't so heavily focused on the bottom line as the business of health care is today. I find in this regard the quote by management consultant Peter Drucker (since elevated to the status of a "major god" of management) amusing: "One reason for the tremendous increase in health care costs in the United States is managerial neglect of the 'hotel services' by the people who dominate the hospital such as doctors and nurses."

Drucker trained as a journalist and became a management guru. I had worked as a journalist to put myself through college and switched to neurosurgery. My perspective on

Drucker's observation is that hospitals in the United States, at least since 1999, have been focusing on "hotel services," which are run by executives and managed primarily by non-nurses and non-doctors.

What have these managerial services contributed to the quality, safety, and efficiency of patient care?

## Trust and Leadership

Trust, even before the pandemic, suffered in all types of and the health care industry was no exception. The supply chain issues of the Covid pandemic exposed the fragmented health care delivery system as well as the unreliability of hospitals and medical supply businesses. The latter's "just-in-time" replenishment system of personal protective equipment (PPE) such as masks, gowns, and gloves was woefully lacking.

Who bears responsibility for the failure to provide PPE to those on the frontline treating pandemic patients?

## The Halo Effect of Leadership

Among the critical few in the analysis of leadership is a hero of mine, Professor Phil Rosenzweig, whose book *The Halo Effect* (2007) provides an incisive revelation of the myths and delusions surrounding leadership.

Professor Rosenzweig lays out the case of how the business management, leadership industries, and their adoring press put forth delusions and reinforce false impressions, in other words, the halo of attribution of an organization's success to those at the top. Nowhere is this more evident than with the CEOs of hospitals.

Hospital CEOs might try to justify their outsized pay packages through their "leadership" and "decision-making" affecting facilities, finance, and supplies. But let's be frank: the most critical decision-making occurs in the clinic or at the bedside, *not* in the wood-paneled conference room.

Saying that patients come to facilities that provide "hotel services" is just one of the delusions produced by this halo effect. It perpetuates the misconception that excellent patient care is the work of the CEO and their executive cadre rather than due to the dedicated practitioners of the profession of the healing arts of nursing, medicine, and the allied health professions of pharmacy, radiology, respiratory care, etc. who are there at the patient's bedside day and night.

When those at the top take credit for those at the bedside, trust is a casualty of the halo effect.

Trust, one of the cornerstones of a relationship, cannot filter down from the top through multiple layers of management, nor can it be created by the glibness of marketing companies spouting sophisms.

Few things personally rankle me more than to be disturbed while watching my favorite sporting event by the marketing ads for hospitals and health systems that pop up. Having been around the block many times, I know what BS is. What a waste of money spent on this type of marketing propaganda that could be better spent on improving patient care.

# Sophisms

*"Never underestimate the difficulty of changing false beliefs by facts."*

—Harvey Rosovsky

*"God preserve us from cunning men and metaphors."*

—Paul Louis Courier de Mere (1773–1825)

Jeremy Bentham (1748–1832), an English philosopher and founder of utilitarianism, believed in producing the greatest happiness for the greatest number of people. As a lawyer and reformer, he advocated for individual and economic freedoms as well as animal rights.

However, Bentham's 1824 collection, *The Book of Fallacies* (London: John and HL Hunt), reveals in stark contrast to his optimistic philosophy the range of false claims and marketing tactics used even during his time.

Today, hospitals use testimonials, metaphors, and slogans to portray themselves as compassionate and caring despite being institutions of industrial medicine, while politicians also compete to exceed the quota for sales pitches.

One of the biggest whoppers involving health care and political sales pitches occurred during the Obamacare sales campaign.

Politifact, the fact-checking website, found thirty-seven variations of the president's remarks on June 6, 2009, that, "If you like the plan you have, you can keep it. If you like the doctor you have, you can keep your doctor too. The only change you'll see are falling costs as our reforms take hold."

Please, if only but for the tragedy of these false promises, hold the laughter.

Although Obamacare was marketed as health care reform, true reform of health care requires both individual and business tradeoffs that must be approved by hospitals and commercial health insurance companies in order to create meaningful changes for the lower cost and improved access and quality of patient care services.

Despite Obamacare's designation as the "Patient Protection and Accountable Care Act" there is little concrete guarantee of improved safety and cost control of health care.

*"The state is the great fiction by which everyone endeavors to live at the expense of everyone else."*

—*Frederic Bastiat (1848)*

Economist Frederic Bastiat (1801–1850) recognized the danger of language cloaked in sophisms, erroneous arguments usually used to deliberately deceive. These half-true, poorly formed arguments and short-sighted expressions obscured the importance of considering all factors in economic decision-making and warned against succumbing to the seductive appeal of oversimplified arguments.

Sophisms of political slogans ignore the basic economic principles that scarcity always exists and that every policy has an opportunity cost. Sound economic reasoning, as noted by Mark Thornton in his 2011 article "Why Bastiat is Still Great," falls victim to oversimplifications that follow the temptations of politicians to just "do something" (Thomas Sowell, 2009).

For example, the recent claim that the expansion of Medicare to include dental, vision, and hearing services in the "Build Back Better" bill would cost nothing. This doozy of a sophism defies economic reality.

## Power Does Not Equal Leadership

*"Power corrupts and absolute power corrupts absolutely."*

—Lord Acton

In health care, those in executive positions such as hospital administrators, CEOs of pharmaceutical and commercial health insurance companies, and departmental heads like deans and clinical chairpersons, hold significant power to control the production and outcomes of their organizations. However, since they have achieved their status by political skill rather than clinical, managerial, or leadership, they have the wrong perspective on priorities of patient care.

Accordingly, in the world of big-box health care, true leadership is mostly if not completely absent, with those in power more concerned with exerting their authority than practicing the virtues of leadership.

This is demonstrated by the enduring question from Machiavelli's *The Prince* (1513). Is it better to be loved or feared?

Unfortunately, as I have learned the hard way, individuals in power often have less hesitation about offending those who people who seek their affection rather than those who aim to instill fear.

The corrupting influence of power on leadership has a detrimental impact on all aspects of health care delivery. Power reaches to the very core of any organization. Power fosters negative behaviors such as arrogance, bullying, and a lack of empathy, ultimately eroding credibility and damaging relationships that are critical to delivering health care.

However, the most disabling side effect of power is the insecurity that it shields and therefore prevents the consideration of ideas for innovation from anyone lower in the food chain than the anointed ones.

(In the July 1, 2023 issue of *The Economist*, health care services job posting were at the bottom of industries mentioning "AI"). As a consequence, innovation takes a back seat to monitoring the bottom line.

The net effect of a business-dominated culture in health care organizations focus on the commoditization of clinical care per business school dogma, shifting away from the mission of patient care.

As a business, the recruitment of health care organization position holders is more and more dependent on head-hunter firms.

In this context, author and journalist Oliver Burkeman's question, "Why do so many mediocre men rise to the top?" is spot on! Burkeman suggests that sexism is a contributing factor. In my more than four decades of experience in hospital care, I have encountered only one female CEO: a sister and former nurse who led a Catholic hospital with the word "mercy" appropriately in its name and mission (sadly it no longer exists).

Psychologist Tomas Chamorro-Premuzic offers an explanation in his book *Who Do So May Incompetent Men Become Leaders (and How to Fix It)*. Chamorro-Premuzic notes that flawed leadership archetypes prioritize "charisma and confidence." These narcissistic individuals frequently seek out positions in "academic" medicine, such as medical school deans and clinical department chairpersons. While they can be easily identified in interviews by asking if they are a narcissist, headhunter search firms minimize these red flags and are not held accountable for their recommendations.

True leaders, those who adhere to duty and obligation to their followers, are rare. The late Sergio Marchionne (1952–2018) was one such inspiring leader. Ms. Marchionne was a CEO who embodied the drive, commitment, and devotion to the mission by which he accomplished not one but two turnarounds of car manufacturers. From all accounts, Marchionne was a servant leader. The story goes that he would fly into a city where one of his company's manufacturing plants was located and would spend his entire trip in the plant working with its management team, sleeping on the couch in the plant managers office.

The automobile industry is reminiscent of the homogeneity that plagues health care, in which one hospital is nearly indistinguishable from another.

This is largely due to the hedgehog-like mentality of hospital CEOs, who are risk-averse and lack transformational leadership skills.

In contrast, Marchionne, a former accountant, philosopher, and lawyer, brought a diverse range of ideas to his role as an inspirational leader in turning around Fiat and Chrysler. As Holman Jenkins noted in a *Wall Street Journal* article, Marchionne recognized that customers desired more than just reliable transportation, and he approached his work with a fox-like adaptability.

In health care, there are no such innovators. Homogeneity of health care executives is the rule. The true value of health care is created on the frontline, not in executive offices.

Therefore, let's put investment into the people who make a difference in patients' lives, not in a marble foyer, an art collection, or a marketing campaign.

To save health care, we need to focus on ways to improve our service, make better decisions, and better communicate recommendations to patients.

In the prior chapter, we spoke of the "invisible hand" as an integral part of health care markets. The "other invisible hand" (LeGrand), apart from consideration of competition affecting delivery of public services, is the rot endemic of those in power of health care. As has been said, a fish starts to rot at the head.

Nowhere is this more obvious than in health care delivery organizations.

# Chapter Twenty

# Ghost Leadership and Zombie Management of Health Care

*"True love is like ghosts which everybody talks about and few have seen."*

—*Francois de la Rochefoucauld (1613–1680, author of* The Moral Maxims and Reflections*)*

What has been said of true love, the same can be said of leadership in health care; both are very rare. Just as true love demands passion and unwavering dedication, true leadership demands a commitment and a constant effort to empower others.

Devotion to the well-being of others is the common mission of love and health care. Many are drawn to the trappings of leadership in health care, but the uneven results in the categories of quality, safety, and accessibility of patient care reflect the shortcomings of those in positions of authority within the health care hierarchy.

Business training (i.e., MBA) and medical school professors are inadequate preparation for leading health care organizations.

Given this context, we must ask: where are the leaders who deploy innovative ideas and tactics to drive improvements in health care? The Covid-19 pandemic has underscored this urgent need for a comprehensive reassessment of the current health care delivery structure. Only by confronting the reality of the systemic failures that the pandemic revealed can we recognize the necessity for true reform.

"The greatest benefit to mankind" as author and historian Roy Porter has called the field of medicine, demands a critical reassessment at all levels.

The progression of medical science has outpaced the ability of its leadership and management to achieve equitable distribution of quality medical care. Consequently, the healing arts are at the mercy of the leadership and management of health care organizations that have become stuck in time. These health care executives and managers are failing us.

David Hurst has identified their problem as being "lost in management thought," a phenomenon that makes it difficult to break free and adopt new approaches to problem-solving required in the post-pandemic world.[38]

This rigidity is a product of the commercialization of business schools to produce a standardized type of manager derived from the study of "historic" cases of businesses.

As supply creates its own demand, the rapid expansion of business schools in the US has kept pace with the growth of

---

[38] Hurst, David: *The New Ecology of Leadership: Business Mastery in a Chaotic World*. Columbia Business School Publishing, NY, 2012

the health care industry. This influx of MBA-credentialed executives and managers, combined with doctors' overwhelming workload, made it easy for professional managers to take over leadership roles in health care.

Similarly, as highlighted in Kenneth and William Hopper's *The Puritan Gift*, a book recounting the Global Financial Crisis of 2008, the rapid rise of professional managers with little or no domain knowledge in banking can lead to disastrous results. When "professional managers" take over, this is a recipe for inefficiency at best and for catastrophy when "black swan" events happen.

*The Puritan Gift* and the pandemic underscore the importance of leaders with domain knowledge. There is no substitute for this.

As the pandemic exposed the weakness in leadership of health care at all levels, and we need alternatives. Health care organizations must cultivate a culture of servant leadership, where the needs of patients and health care workers take precedence over executive self-interest.

What are the obstacles to servant leadership? Let's identify and understand the key players in the health care industry who are responsible for perpetuating its inequities. On the delivery side, these include hospital CEOs, VPs, clinical department chairs, and directors of clinical service lines.

The health care industry's financial landscape is also rife with challenges, driven in large part by the influence of politicians who cater to those who hold positions of power within commercial health insurance companies. Crony capitalism pervades the relationships in Washington, D.C. among the Congress and health care industry lobbyists.

# The "Visible Hand" of Management in Health Care Organizations

Professor Alfred Chandler's book *The Visible Hand* is a supportive reference for understanding the management of the production and distribution of goods and services in the United States. Although not explicitly stated, this work provides a foundation for the health care–industrial complex.

Professor Chandler presents the rationale behind the development of hierarchical structures inherent in all business organizations. The growth of hospital executive and administrative hierarchies has grown lockstep with the expansion of medical technology, capital investment, and the requirement of handling accompanying transaction costs for medical care. The economists Coase, Pauly, and Madden anticipated the formation of firms for this purpose, and management of financial transactions becomes a larger and larger part of their operations.

Accordingly, the growth of hospital hierarchies required an increasing number of individuals with financial transactional skills who have no requirement of medical knowledge. As in non-medical businesses, these administrative personnel were described as "The Organization Man" by William Whyte (1956) and "Transaction Man" by Nicholas Lemann in 2019. These types of individuals owe their jobs to their non-clinical bosses.

In 1941, James Burnham warned of the potential for professional business bureaucrats to become the ruling class in modern society, a prescient observation that has come to fruition in organizations involved in patient care. Rather than a perspective of medical care as "the greatest benefit to mankind" (Porter), these denizens of administration and management of health care organizations are part of a business. This takeover of medicine by business management bureaucracies plagues frontline health care providers seeking approval for medication, tests, or procedures from pharmacy benefit managers and third-party payers. These bureaucratic enterprises serve as gatekeepers for cost control, prioritizing their own benefit over the value of patient care.

Doctors face additional obstacles to patient care imposed upon them by their own peers. What less welcome phrase is there for a physician than a "peer-to-peer" conference to justify a recommended test or procedure for their patient?

As the health care–industrial complex becomes increasingly focused on cost control, i.e., increased profit for health insurance companies, doctors are finding themselves at the forefront of scrutiny for approval of treatment plans. These tactics not only devalue the role of the physician but also commoditize patient care, reducing it to a mere transactional encounter. Those of us who value the humanistic experiences and knowledge of the healing arts understand that patient care is far more valuable than the direction that the business interests of the health care–industrial complex are taking us.

The zombies of the health care executive suite and their enslaved managers must not be allowed to continue to pick the brains of nurses and doctors to pretend that they are part of the true value of patient care.

## Chapter Twenty-One

## Strategy in Health Care: What is it and Why So Complicated?

According to a 2017 report by Alex Kacik in *Modern Healthcare*, the largest pay increases for executives in the health care industry were awarded to those in the position of chief strategy officer. It's admirable that these individuals are able to provide for their families and invest in their children's education.

However, it's worth noting that the strategies employed by these health care systems, which may also be informed by expensive consultant advice, are often recycled from outdated "monopoly" playbooks. This approach not only wastes valuable resources but also reflects the inability of hospital systems to move beyond traditional models due to leadership inertia and a reluctance to embrace change. This reluctance stems from a lack of incentives to abandon existing practices as well as apprehension about the unknown future.

The businesses that provide medical services follow, as do all businesses, strategies and tactics that create demand for their services and supply them at a price that will keep them in business. Simple enough. However, the health care industry, which primarily includes hospitals and their suppliers, pharmaceutical companies, and insurance providers, operates in a unique context. These businesses are responsible for delivering medical services, and as such, their operations are heavily influenced by federal government programs like Medicare, Medicaid, and Obamacare, as well as other initiatives like Tricare, which provides care for military personnel and their dependents. This dynamic creates a complex interplay between the demands of the market and the regulations imposed by the government, which must be carefully navigated to ensure the provision of high-quality care while also achieving business objectives.

The intersection of these various health care entities unfortunately results in a highly complex delivery system that can be challenging for patients and medical professionals to navigate. As described by Relman, this system represents a "medical–industrial complex" that combines various businesses involved in the diagnosis and treatment of illness. These businesses invest in the necessary technology to provide care and set prices for their services based on a cost-benefit analysis and profit-loss strategy that prioritizes financial gain over other considerations. Ultimately, this results in a health care system that is run like a business, with the primary goal of maximizing profits.

As with most businesses, health care utilizes advertising and marketing as part of its strategy to differentiate from competitors. Risk management is another component of health care, and all of these support functions of the business of patient care, which can use disruptive innovation to create value.

Economists may also be so bold as to weigh in.[39]

Before the onset of the Covid-19 pandemic, health care in the United States was primarily driven by the interests of hospitals, health insurance companies, and related businesses, such as pharmaceuticals, medical technology (including electronic medical records and big data analytics), medical device manufacturers, supply chain vendors, and financial institutions. In order to gain a competitive edge in the market, hospitals pursued a strategy of expanding their networks or systems through horizontal mergers with other hospitals and acquiring physician practices. This approach, which follows the Michael Porter paradigm for strategic planning, was intended to enhance the market position of hospitals and provide them with greater leverage over health care providers and insurers.

By pursuing this strategy of horizontal integration, large hospital systems aimed to gain a competitive advantage by expanding their reach and providing access to health care for a larger population. This, in turn, would increase their leverage in negotiations with third-party payers, such as commercial health insurance providers and federal programs like Medicare and Obamacare. Additionally, these hospital systems aimed to build robust population health components, as required by Obamacare, while simultaneously developing endogenous big data to support patient care and commercial objectives. In this way, these big-box hospital systems sought to establish a dominant position in the health care marketplace by leveraging their scale and influence over both providers and payers.

---

39   Porter, Michael E. and Lee, Thomas H. "The Strategy That Will Fix Healthcare." *Harvard Business Review*, October 2013.

It's worth noting that hospital systems are not the only entities focused on leveraging big data in health care. This is evidenced by the acquisition of Optum, a commercial health care information aggregator, by United Healthcare, the largest commercial health insurer. This move underscores the growing importance of big data in the health care industry, as well as the desire of industry leaders to capture and leverage this data to gain a competitive edge.

Another example of strategic mergers aimed at combining disparate components of the health care industry's value chain is the recent merger between Aetna, the third-largest health insurer, and CVS, a company that operates retail pharmacies, on-site clinics, and a pharmacy benefit management business. This type of vertical merger, as described by Dafny,[40] represents an alternative approach to building strategic advantage in the health care industry by bringing together previously siloed entities in a single integrated system. By doing so, companies like Aetna and CVS aim to streamline the delivery of health care services, improve patient outcomes, and reduce costs.

As the famous boxer Mike Tyson once said, "Everyone has a plan until they get punched in the mouth." The Covid-19 pandemic has undoubtedly been a devastating blow to the health care industry, forcing leaders to reassess their strategies and priorities in light of unprecedented challenges. With so much uncertainty and disruption, it is more important than ever for health care organizations to adapt and evolve their strategies to meet the needs of patients, providers, and communities in this rapidly changing landscape. The

---

40    Dafny, LS: "Does CVS-Aetna Spell the End of Business as Usual?" *NEJM* 387(7): 593-595. 2018

question remains: what is the path forward for the health care industry?

The late Colin S. Gray (1943–2020), an esteemed expert on strategy, outlined the importance of strategy in his work, *The Future of Strategy*. He argued that strategy serves as a means of controlling action to achieve a desired political effect while also accounting for the ever-present threat of chaos that can disrupt even the best-laid plans. In essence, strategic thinking is essential for organizations to navigate the complex and unpredictable environments in which they operate and to achieve objectives while minimizing risk and uncertainty.

The Covid-19 pandemic has had a profound impact on the health care industry, disrupting its delivery operations and financing. As a result, elective surgeries were put on hold, and primary care, including preventive and diagnostic services, was postponed. However, this disruption has also created opportunities for innovation, particularly in the realm of technology. For instance, the pandemic has accelerated the adoption of telehealth consultations, which has reduced administrative tasks such as data entry on electronic medical records and allowed health care professionals to focus on more meaningful tasks.

The intersection of strategy and politics, which gave rise to the health care–industrial complex, has also been significantly impacted by the Covid-19 pandemic. The question now is whether the status quo will persist. It is essential to learn from the lessons of the 2008–2009 Great Financial Crisis, during which the concept of "too big to fail" prevailed, and ensure that Congress does not continue to engage in crony capitalism with the health care–industrial complex.

Providing financial support to hospitals during the Covid-19 pandemic was undoubtedly essential (CARES Act); however, it sends the wrong message to hospital systems seeking to augment their market power[41] (ref: Lake Forest Hospital). This approach is reminiscent of the classic strategy that aims to win the previous battle. The failure to innovate patient care and the perpetuation of traditional health care strategies stem from the stagnant bureaucracies entrenched within existing organizations, plagued by what William F. Miller called "the tyranny of dead ideas."[42]

The health care industry's hierarchical organizations are constrained by their inability to adapt, despite the interplay between strategy and politics in health care delivery (e.g., Medicare/Medicaid/Obamacare). Hospitals and commercial health insurance providers, despite their executive salaries, find themselves in a Faustian bargain with government health care programs (e.g., Medicare/Medicaid, Obamacare). Unfortunately, patients and health care providers are at a disadvantage due to the limited scale of their influence compared to the vast resources of health care companies, including their lobbyists and accountants.

---

41   Dorfman, Daniel I. "Pandemic a factor as Lake Forest Hospital officials start expansion process; 'The volume of patients (shows) ... we need to plan for the next phase of evolution.'" *Chicago Tribune*, January 29, 2002.

42   Miller, Matt. *The Tyranny of Dead Ideas: Letting Go of the Old Ways of Thinking to Unleash a New Prosperity*. Times Books, Henry Holt & Company, New York, 2009.

The federal government has implemented Centers for Medicare and Medicaid programs, which have adopted "hierarchical payment models."[43] These models reduce the patient–doctor relationship to soulless "episodes" determined by metrics that defy measurement. The tragedy of these programmatic mandates is felt by both patients and doctors, who are trapped in a Faustian bargain with commercial health insurance companies that serve as the gatekeepers of health care encounters.

Unfortunately, the government's failure to enact genuine quality, safety, and cost measures has left insurance companies to shoulder the burden of ensuring quality. This approach is insufficient and fails to serve patients to the standards they deserve. A radical approach to strategy that maximizes value in health care is needed to rise above these half-measures. It will require leadership with the will to make difficult decisions, as Nietzsche observed. Despite the glowing profit reports from "big box" chains, the sustainability of health care will require radical changes that go beyond the status quo.

---

43   Shrank, William H., Chernew, Michael E., and Navathe, Amol S. "Hierarchical Payment Models-A Path for Coordinating Population- and Episode-Based Payment Models." *Journal of the American Medical Association*, 2022 Feb 1;327(5):423-424. doi: 10.1001/jama.2021.23786.

# Chapter Twenty-Two

# Lessons of the Pandemic: The Price of Panic

Any illusions about the capability of the most complicated government–business conglomerate in the world that provides health care in the United States should be put to rest by the tragedy of the Covid pandemic.

The United States health care system was not alone.

The Covid-19 pandemic exposed the vulnerability of health care worldwide to disruption. The pandemic-induced health care breakdown mirrored societal breakdown and led to panic. Some of the most notable features included:

1. The pandemic produced, on a global scale, a situation of "multi-organ" failure in health care systems mirroring the effect on patients who succumbed to the virus.

2. The "multi-organ" failure of health care systems involved its leadership, management, delivery, and training. This was a direct result of the inability of each of these components to adapt to rare and unexpected events, commonly known as "black swan" events.

This failure reflected numerous deficiencies in health care systems, hampered by constipated decision-making, groupthink, and control in the hands of bureaucrats who dominate health care organizations.

3. The ill-conceived total economic shutdown as a response to the pandemic forced governments worldwide to rely on traditional economic tools of the supply-side variety dating back to economist Maynard Keynes from the 1930s. Unfortunately, these tools had the unintended consequence of imitating rip-roaring inflation with no end in sight.

   The ongoing inflation battle, stimulated by pandemic supply-side economics, will further challenge health care costs.

   Who will bear the rising costs of health care fueled by inflation?

4. The pandemic shock of "creative destruction"[44] magnified the inequality of access to safe, high-quality health care in the United States and throughout the world. This can be a positive thing if innovation is unleashed to address this criminal deficiency.

5. The human toll of the pandemic must not be forgotten. The lack of preparedness and the failure of leadership must be accounted for in order to make a fitting memorial to those who died and to prevent tragedy in the future.

6. The Covid-19 pandemic was often the tragic reality of people dying alone in ICU beds, isolated from their loved

---

44   Economist Joseph Schumpter coined the phrase "creative destruction" in his 1942 book *Capitalism, Socialism, and Democracy*.

ones. This reality is a stark reminder of the impact of inequality on those who have lost their lives during the pandemic. It is inexcusable and reprehensible that such conditions persist, and we must take action to ensure that they never happen again.

As a tribute to the memories of those who lost their lives, we must renew our commitment to humanism in all aspects of medical care. This requires a fundamental shift in the way we deliver medical care, with a focus on empathy, compassion, and respect for the dignity of all patients.

Inequalities in health care safety, quality, efficiency, and cost must be addressed, and resources must be allocated to ensure that all patients receive equitable care, regardless of their socioeconomic status of background. Only through a renewed commitment to humanism can we honor the memories of those who have lost their lives and ensure that future generations receive the care they deserve.

In the wake of the pandemic, we have a unique opportunity to transform the health care system into one that is truly patient-centered and compassionate. Let us seize this opportunity and commit ourselves to the noble pursuit of humanism in medical care.

7. According to Fleisher, et al.,[45] patient safety deteriorated during the pandemic. The confined reliance on "checklists" and adoption of technology to prevent "never

---

45 Fleisher, et al. "Health Care Safety during the Pandemic and Beyond – Building a System that Ensures Resilience." *New England Journal of Medicine*, 386 (7): 609–611, 2022.

events," such as amputating the wrong extremity or removing the wrong organ, must be adopted immediately.

As such, as we emerge from the pandemic, it is clear that there is a priority to improve safety and quality of health care. The failure of health care organizations to commit to patient safety as a priority can no longer be tolerated.

It is imperative that health care organizations stop paying lip service to patient safety and prioritize patient safety with proactive steps to prevent adverse events. The "checklist manifesto" was enacted in 2011, and has become somewhat outmoded. There are more up-to-date innovative technology platforms for surgical safety, for instance SafeStartMedical.com.

8. And last but certainly not least, the Covid-19 pandemic put horrendous stress on all nursing and medical personnel on the frontlines. Burnout was already a significant problem for health care professionals prior to the pandemic. In the wake of Covid, "more than half of health care workers stressed, overworked, and ready to leave," according to a survey led by Brigham and Women's Hospital investigators.

9. Returning to the status quo post-pandemic will not help those so affected by burnout.

The Covid-19 pandemic was unique in many ways, from the "mysterious" appearance of a novel virus that triggered a global economic disaster through widespread lockdowns, to the rapid development of Covid vaccines. Human nature, being what it is, brought out the best and worst in us.

The legacy of the pandemic will be felt for years to come, not only in economic terms but also in its effect on the delivery of health care. Health care workers, were pushed to their limits, resulting in burnout and exhaustion. This, in turn, has further eroded trust in our health care institutions as with other institutions of society.

It is critical to recognize that the pandemic has exposed the fragility of our institutions and the need for a renewed commitment to trust and transparency from leadership. Health care organizations, governments, and other institutions must work together to rebuild trust and restore confidence.

The Coronavirus ultimately revealed the high cost of economic globalization and extended supply chains failing to provide even the most rudimentary yet critical necessities of gloves, gowns, and masks. This merits recrimination.

The heroes of the frontline of health care contrast mightily with the vacuum of global leadership. This leadership vacuum was demonstrative of ignorance and outright panic on full display by so-called "experts" who were either outright frauds or bumbling incompetents at best. Some of them sought to capitalize on the pandemic by producing books on their supposed "leadership," showing their extreme self-interest and egotism rather than living up to their duty of effective leadership. Given how feebly our public health government warning systems performed at all levels, taking bows for leadership during the pandemic is rich indeed.

At this critical juncture, it is imperative to treasure the knowledge gleaned from the sacrifices of so many made during the pandemic.

There are many more lessons to be learned from over 1.2 million deaths in the United States and greater than 5 million worldwide. While the mortality figure pales in comparison to the estimated greater than 50 million deaths in the flu pandemic of 1918, the results in 2020–2023 are nothing to be proud of for any politician, policymaker, or health care executive. The real test for the future will be the handling of the repercussions of the pandemic on society. For one thing, the loss by burnout of the frontline nurses and doctors. How will they be replaced?

What other lessons can we learn from this unprecedented wake-up call? John Barry of Tulane University School of Public Health and Tropical Medicine and author of *The Great Influenza: The Story of the Deadliest Pandemic in History*, poses the question of how a pandemic ends and reminds us that the outcome hinges on the virus itself. Will we acknowledge the weakening of our health care–industrial complex to prepare for future pandemics, or will we continue to follow the pattern of the US military–industrial complex, fighting the last war and returning to the status quo?

# Chapter Twenty-Three

# Dumbing Down Health Care

*"Don't read books on medicine; a misprint may kill you."*
—*Mark Twain*

Most health care delivery organization's executives, despite clinging to outdated business models and illusions, were unaffected by the massive disruption to society caused by the Covid-19 pandemic. Not having "skin in the game" as patients, nurses, and doctors did, these executives were insulated from the tragedy.

Consequently, there is little incentive on the part of health care executives to re-evaluate their organizations and business models. While similar in precedent to the banks being "too big to fail" that survived the Great Financial Crisis of 2007–2008, without a change in their ways, our health care remains weakened and susceptible to the next big shock that comes its way.

As such, despite the pandemic wake-up call, health care delivery organizations continue to pursue a strategy of "Big

Med" system expansion through mergers and acquisitions, and they continue applying archaic operational models to patient care.

Denning[46] identified four categories of flaws with this approach. First, there is the risk of asking the wrong question altogether. Is health care similar to ordering off the menu of a fast-food restaurant? Someone has had the brilliant idea that "consumer-driven" health care for an "informed consumer" will help provide clarity and a more valuable decision-making process for improving access, quality and cost of patient care. Keep dreaming.

As consumers, we generally think more is better, which is not necessarily the case with health care.

Also, should you pick your brain surgeon off of one of the consumer survey sites?

Second, there is a mismatch between the knowledge mode in this case the business school process, with the nature of patient care. Patient care critically depends upon establishing communication between the patient and provider that occurs potentially under the most stressful circumstances. Building the trust that is an essential component of this communication affects all other parts of the decision-making process for health care. How does business management factor into the patient-care relationship?

Third, the management model for building care may be ill-suited for the unique challenges of health care. People are not light trucks, so how does the Toyota production system apply to patient care?

---

46  Dafny, LS: "Does CVS-Aetna Spell the End of Business as Usual?" *NEJM* 387(7): 593-595. 2018

And finally, there is a risk of drawing the wrong conclusions about scaling, as what works in one industry may not necessarily work in health care.[47]

The reality is that the comparison of patient care to ordering cheesecake or building trucks is simply not valid. Patient care is customized to each patient. As Francis Peabody said in The Care of the Patient, the secret of the care of the patient is in caring for the patient. Management of this requirement is a humanistic and not business function.

Granted that hospitals with their high capital costs and costs of maintenance, operations, and labor are exceedingly complex to manage. These factors do provide a rationale for a greater reliance on business school types and lawyers to handle finances and regulations.

However, business must never distract from the mission and focus of hospitals to improve competency, safety and quality of patient care.

Innovation in risk management and improvement in clinical-decision-making are the areas with the greatest potential for improving patient care.

Unfortunately, the bloated bureaucracies of hospital management have become increasingly disconnected from this mission. Instead of focusing on the critical responsibility

---

[47] As an example, the suggestion of Boston surgeon and *New Yorker* writer Atul Gawande suggests in his article "Big Med" that the national chain restaurant, The Cheesecake Factory, is a model for the kind of standardization and quality that have been lacking in health care. He argues that their model for delivering "delicious meals" represents the kind of affordable, reliable product that would better fit the budgets of cost-conscious health care while meeting the needs of their *customers*–in the competitive new world of medicine.

of supporting value in patient care, hospital management is often bogged down by endless meetings and transaction processing costs.

Management guru Peter Drucker observed that hospitals were originally driven by a mission to provide the best possible patient care. They were also once considered "learning organizations," a concept further defined by Peter Senge in *The Fifth Discipline: The Art and Practice of The Learning Organization* (1990). Learning organizations prioritize tapping into people's capacity and commitment to learn at all levels and focusing on creating value for their customers that sets themselves apart from competitors. However, I have observed a shift in academic medical centers from a focus on bedside teaching to the pursuit of translational research. As such, simply being a "great teaching hospital" is no longer enough to differentiate a brand in today's health care landscape.

## Will the Amazonians Take Over Health Care?

Artificial intelligence and machine learning are the great unknowns influencing patient care. The question of whether health care will be dominated by AI-focused businesses like Amazon or Walmart, for example, is a real concern.

The supply chains of Amazon and Walmart outshine those of hospitals, as evidenced by the tragic shortage of masks, gloves, and gowns in hospital-managed supply chains during the pandemic.

However, the idea of ordering a book for a "DIY" appendectomy is concerning. It's worth noting that Amazon-Berkshire-JP

Morgan attempted to disrupt health care with Haven, an entity that ceased operations after three years in January 2021. Despite this, it's unlikely that corporations will give up on the $4 trillion prize that is US health care. For example, Amazon has recently announced a new health care delivery initiative, and private equity investment firms are increasingly on the lookout for health care service opportunities.

We don't want health care to fall further under the not-so-tender mercies of "big tech" or the "get rich quick" mantra of private equity. It's time to wake up from the delusions of who controls our health care.

## Chapter Twenty-Four

# What Would Success in Health Care Reform Even Look Like?

*"If many remedies are prescribed for an illness, you may be certain that the illness has no cure."*
—*Anton Chekhov,* The Cherry Orchard

*"Never underestimate the difficulty of changing false beliefs by facts."*
—*Henry Rosovsky, American Economist*

It is clear that the current state of delivery of health care, heavily dependent on transfer payments from the federal government and legacy delivery models, is not a picture of health care reform. Obamacare, as with many other federally mandated programs, constructs devilishly complicated rules for delivering value without a clear concept of what value truly represents. Yet it does little to forestall the reality of inequality of access to safe, high-quality patient care services.

It's clear that true reform of the inequality that is causing health care to fail requires a radically different approach than what is currently in place. Ways to hold every component of the health care industry accountable, to improving access to a more sustainable and equitable system, demands accepting the reality of the waste in the $4 trillion dollar health care economy.

If markets, the foundation of capitalism, are a mechanism for producing efficiency and lower costs, then why is health care delivery in the US such a fiasco? It's because the biggest challenges to the reform of health care are the multitude of special interests that support the present structure for delivering health care. Crony capitalism corrupts competition to improve health care.

Crony capitalism in health care centers on the unholy alliance of hospitals, commercial health insurance, and CMS (Centers for Medicare & Medicade Services). Hospitals are relics of a bygone era of patient care. By virtue of their management bureaucracies, hospitals today represent the inertia that produces unsustainability on account of the inability to manage the complexity of clinical imperatives, while simultaneously adopting innovation that is critical for their and their patients' survival.

Enrico Coiera, an Australian computer scientist and medical informatics researcher, has written extensively on the intersection of technology and health care, especially in regard to the challenges of integrating clinical and administrative systems. Dr. Coiera observes that the existence of parallel clinical and health administrative systems creates redundant management bureaucracies as well as non-aligned support entities and distinct jargon that hinder constructive communication and strategic agendas. Attempting to bridge the divide between these clinical and administrative "tribes" with simplistic offerings by consultants fails to recognize the deep division between those on the frontline and those in management positions. In my experience as a surgeon for over thirty years, it is literally speaking a foreign language to administrators, many of whom have the only connection to humanity as that of occupying a body.

In the face of competing cultures of medicine and administration, "fixing health care" will require heroic leadership to bring together these "tribes" and foster collaboration. (AI offers the hope of eliminating the functions of some of these administrative zombies. Godspeed, Dr. Coiera!)

## The COVID Pandemic Has Changed Patient Care Forever! (If we will only accept that!)

The ultimate reality following the Covid-19 pandemic will play out over the next few years. As such, we cannot predict how health care will transpire. One thing we must ensure is that hospital and health insurance company CEOs do not dictate health care's future. These executives, even in the face of the pandemic tragedy, will always resort to the status quo bias that protects their position. Their lack of incentive to change or ability to put in place innovation for future patient care stops at the walls of their brick-and-mortar barricades. Deviations from their established business models are a threat to their self-interests. And Obamacare, enacted in 2010, only reinforces this status quo. Million-dollar salaries of hospital executives do nothing but reinforce complacency.

Instead of Obamacare that has reinforced the imbalance of power weighted in favor of hospitals and insurance companies, a power grab that only exacerbated health care inequality, but it has also eroded trust. We need to create programs that actually ensure excellent health care. Technology companies offer "without walls" business models that can bring health care directly to the consumer without the "middlemen and women" of administration.

The Covid pandemic should serve as a humbling reminder that the primary goal of patient care is to alleviate suffering and provide comfort to the sick as the primary focus of any health care organization. This mission is only fulfilled by supporting those professionals who learn trust through commitment to the healing arts of nursing and medicine.

The power of executives insulated from this commitment was exposed during the pandemic, while the commitment of the frontline staff of nurses and doctors was on full display. As such, the power for transformation from "business as usual" back to improving access, quality, safety, and controlling costs—in essence, a radical transformation of the medical-industrial complex—is not only necessary; it is critical to the survival of what patient care should be.

## Chapter Twenty-Five

# Diagnosis and Cure: The Business Transformation of American Medicine

In the words of one of my esteemed mentors, the late Orville T. Bailey, M.D., a renowned neuropathologist, a mere glance through the microscope at a tumor specimen was enough for him to declare, "A blind man with a stick could make this diagnosis." It was that clear-cut.

As for health care, the diagnosis is likewise "a mess." What is abundantly clear is that the current configuration of the health care–industrial complex is unsustainable. The diagnosis comes from the evidence that significant benefits to quality of life in the United States from birth to death are stationary or retreating despite the ever-growing cost. It's a story of misplaced incentives and focus on treatment that tangentially influence the quality of life. Essentially, health care is an example of market economics gone awry. Others would further call out the primacy of financial self-interest in health care as pure and simple greed.[48]

Health care, which comprises many businesses that provide care to the sick, has unfortunately become tainted and, some like Dr. Berwick would say, despoiled by the pursuit of profit over the best care of patients. As a result, health care providers sometimes cater to conditions that are not truly illnesses or that are only tangentially related to illness. This market-motivated approach has corrupted the professionalism of the healing arts and splintered the patient–doctor relationship. This emphasis on profit obscures attempts to make real progress toward safer patient care.

According to Professor Coyle and Joseph Schumpeter's theory of "creative destruction," competitive markets should drive innovation, the development of new goods and services, and economic growth. However, principal business models in health care, hospitals, and commercial health insurance companies are more interested in inhibiting competition than investing in improved delivery. While economists love competition, businesses tend to avoid it. Incumbents in health care seek to keep new entrants out, thus maintaining their dominance.

In many states, hospital "certificate of need" committees serve as gatekeepers, limiting competition from doctor-owned ambulatory surgery centers and other potential competitors. These committees are stuffed with political cronies of hospitals. Hospitals aim to prevent their most productive surgeons from leaving to establish their own facilities. This practice adds to the dysfunctional market that controls health care in the United States.

---

48    Berwick, Donald M. "Salve Lucrum: The Existential Threat of Greed in US Health Care," *JAMA Network*, January 2023.

While actual patient care, which is delivered by health care professionals, is based on relationships; business relationships are based on cronyism and politics. Trust is a crucial component of the patient–nurse–physician relationship. This is not the case in the business world. Measures such as the Trust Barometer Index for business continue to record low levels. Unfortunately, as business took over patient care, health care could not be "immunized" against the trust deficit endemic to business.

## The Cure:
## Table 2

**The Cure for Inequality of Access, Safety, Quality, and Cost of Patient Care:**

- Accept reality and all its myths and fallacies.

- "New Economics" (Diane Coyle).

- True "meaningful use" of technology (*not* data entry of electronic medical records).

- Decision-making enhanced by artificial intelligence, bringing about elimination of "grinding functions" of health care administration that are a time and money sink.

- Risk-management that improves safety by meaningful dynamic platforms (SafeStartMedical.com) that are proactive at the point of care.

- A leadership platform that serves all constituents of patient care.

"Delenda Est Carthago" ("Carthage Must be Destroyed")

To improve the current health care system, nothing short of total disruption is required. As the Romans said, "Carthage must be destroyed." Optimizing decision-making using platform-based artificial intelligence and automated intelligence-driven ecosystems will deliver true value (*Deep Medicine*, Dr. Eric Topal). This will require a radical shift away from control of medical care by the toxic hierarchies. A new ecology that creates opportunities for enhanced safety and quality of decision-making will curtail waste and improve utilization and efficiency of patient care.

The health care industry has been wasting resources even before the pandemic hit. This is a function of outdated business models, bureaucratic management, and a lack of innovation and authentic leadership. Leadership of health care is driven by surveys based on survivor bias. Survivor bias distorts our view of the past. It leads to overconfidence in the future and prevents us from truly learning from past mistakes.[49]

## New Economics of Health Care

Economist Thomas Sowell warned that, in economics, it's not about finding solutions but rather about making tradeoffs. This comment is an anathema to the US Congress, which persists in a high-wire act with the nation's finances. Congress's ignorance of actual return on spending on health care services through Medicare/Medicaid/Obamacare invites the health care–industrial complex to interpret how health care

---

[49] Lockwood, David. *Fooled by the Winners: How Survivor Bias Deceives Us.* Greenleaf Book Group Press, 2021

gets done. Their slice of the health care pie is delicious, no doubt, especially when accountability is buried in complexity.

While the US government sets the political agenda and funds over sixty percent of health care, hospital systems and commercial health insurance companies primarily determine how to meet these objectives. Meanwhile, the frontline of health care nurses and doctors must navigate a variety of obstacles, such as regulations and cumbersome electronic medical records, in order to deliver actual patient care.

In 2023, the policies of government and the control by the private sector (health care–industry complex) impact all of us.

I know from over thirty-five years on the frontline that the most significant value in health care is generated by the patient–nurse/doctor relationship. This relationship creates the foundation for decision-making and ultimately determines the value of health care, yet its value continues to be corrupted by business.

## Restoring Value to Health Care

Rather than treating health care as a market, which it is not, we should focus on providing individuals with the right information to make informed decisions about their health. By doing so, we can shift the balance of power away from financial interests and restore the privacy and importance of the patient–nurse/doctor relationship. This will involve nurses and doctors to be radically committed to recusing patient care.

In order to improve medical decision making, we need to provide nurses and doctors with technology that frees them from the constraints of electronic medical records (EMR) and provides valuable cognitive support through artificial intelligence (AI).

The cure, as stated previously, depends on enhancing everyone's health based on true value.

In the ongoing struggle to gain control over health care, there is a need to recognize and appreciate the value of nursing and medical professions in providing humanistic care to the sick. This battle is comparable to the Roman legion's victory over Carthage, which was deemed impossible but necessary to save the Roman Empire. The Social Transformation of Medicine (Starr) and Mankind's Greatest Benefit (Porter) emphasize the importance of patient care over the commercial objectives of the medical–industrial complex. The business transformation of medicine is not the right model.

The Covid-19 pandemic of 2019–2020 has highlighted the significant flaws in the current health care system, which prioritizes business and science over the humanistic aspect of patient care. While tragic, this unfortunate situation presents an opportunity to innovate and improve patient care to meet the needs of all.

# Chapter Twenty-Six

## Value/Quality/Cost/Efficiency: Are We Measuring the Critical Needs of Patient Care?

In 1926, physician and Harvard Medical School professor Francis Peabody delivered a landmark address to the students titled "The Care of the Patient." He emphasized the significance of the doctor–patient relationship and the importance of compassion in medical practice. The very heart of the healing arts of patient care is just that: caring for the patient. It is here, in this fundamental understanding and responsibility, where all of the triumphs, disasters, waste, miracles, and even the pervasive influence of business interests sanctioned by government intervention reside. The age-old adage that "value is in the eye of the beholder" has never been more relevant than in this fundamental basis of health care. All other aspects of the interaction of the patient with their physician (or nurse, physician assistant, pharmacist, etc.) are just a distraction. Unfortunately, the distractions imposed by the government, health insurance, health care facility management, etc. are substantial and have caused an imbalance that fosters inequality in safety, quality, and other measures of value of health care.

## The Value Paradox

The value paradox, that is, what comprises true value of health care, is a contest between a patient and their health care provider and the business objectives of profit. Defining value in patient care goes well beyond a simple equation that equates value with the ratio of quality to cost (value = quality/cost) as some would hold.[50] Other measures to define value have been constructed, such as the International Classification of Diseases (ICD-10) and the Resource-Based Relative Value Scale (RBRVS). Each of these systems, however, are deeply flawed and susceptible to manipulation and abuse.

While a patient makes a determination of the value based on their encounters with nurses, physicians, pharmacists, emergency rooms, etc. and how they make them feel, it is another thing when they receive the bill for services because it makes them reconsider the value they received.

Value of patient care is a battle between emotion and finances.

This commoditization of health care, as a service that is linked to a third party, can create significant friction in the relationship key to creating value for the patient. For example, as a neurosurgeon, I understand that not everyone in my neighborhood with low back pain needs to seek my expertise. Nevertheless, with a few brief exchanges and focused questioning, I can usually diagnose the issue and

---

50   Porter, Michael E. "What is Value in Healthcare?" *The New England Journal of Medicine*, 2010

recommend effective treatment. The question then becomes, what is the value in terms of reassurance of that service to the person seeking relief from their back pain?

## What Is the Quality of Quality Measurement?

Quality measures are standard practice in patient care today. These proxies for assessing quality of care are part and parcel of third-party payers' assessments of physicians' performance.

Also, Medicare via a survey, the HCAHPS (Hospital Consumer Assessment of Health Care Provider Systems), is a twenty-nine-item survey that enables patients to give feedback on their hospital experience. It is then linked to reimbursement for hospital services through the Hospital Value-Based Purchasing Program. Could anyone have ever devised a more convoluted way to understand the true value of patient care? As with all consumer surveys, quality is brought with emotional baggage.

Quality assessment, in addition, has spawned an entire sub-industry that includes "experts" certified in quality from academic institutions or retired physicians looking to supplement their lifestyles by "Monday morning quarterbacking" of the efforts of those still in the arena.

Hospitals have been using their lobbyists to hinder the disclosure of their care costs, including their facilities' direct and indirect costs and management fees. This lack of transparency in hospital pricing has long plagued economists. For example, the infamous $100 charge for one pill of aspirin.

Safety and innovative risk management affecting decision-making are also essential determinants of value that receive lip service from health care executives. Like Mom's Thanksgiving stuffing, safety in patient care is spoken of in glowing terms. The reality is that only the patient, the patient's family, and the patient's doctors have the most skin in the game, and all want the safest outcome. The alternative reality is that safety involves many more individuals and parts that provide its value.

## Value

The most formidable obstacle to rectifying the deficiencies in the provision of health care services, which account for the unequal access, uneven safety and quality, and runaway cost, is the determination of value. By improving safety and decision-making.

Value is defined as quality (safe + timely care) divided by cost (decision-making).

The other part of value is the redistribution of funding. To put it simply, those who take from the funds allocated for patient care outnumber those who give, and they extract value before any care is provided. This includes hospital administrators and insurance company executives who extract more value than the health care providers who actually deliver care, such as nurses, doctors, pharmacists, and respiratory therapists. Patients and their families value the care these providers give, but the health care–industrial complex has rigged the system in their favor, similar to how defense contractors have rigged the military–industrial complex. One solution would be to require all aspects of patient care to demonstrate their contribution to value, just as doctors are required to do.

Let's begin by fostering a culture of accountability and responsibility for patient care safety, quality, efficiency, and cost across the entire health care delivery system. To tackle the headwinds of waste that hinder progress toward eliminating health care inequality, we must first categorize the value evaluation process, drawing inspiration from Professor Mariana Mazzucato's book *The Value of Everything: Making and Taking in the Global Economics* (2018), to clarify who provides what to the process.

To achieve this, we need to define what we mean by "value" in patient care services. It is not simply a matter of Relative Value Units (RVUs), Current Procedural Terminalogy (CPT) codes, or oversimplified equations like "value = quality/cost", which can be easily misinterpreted and widely varied in their application.

As we have previously discussed, attempting to quantify quality and cost as separate, mythical creatures can be counterproductive to the true value of the patient–doctor encounter. Instead, we need to focus on the unique qualities and interactions that make each patient encounter valuable, rather than relying on predetermined measures.

In my experience as a surgeon, I have often found myself providing value to patients through empathetic communication and explanation saving them from unnecessary surgery. Unfortunately, the current evaluation and management (E&M) codes in the CPT register fail to account for this valuable service and the cost-saving from avoiding unnecessary surgery.

The codes for patient care instead prioritize tangible actions over meaningful discussions, which cannot be adequately captured by simply documenting information in the electronic medical record (EMR).

To determine true value in patient care, we must draw upon a variety of disciplines, including political economics, behavioral economics, and innovative risk management strategies, rather than relying on simplistic checklists such as ordering a CBC (complete blood count) or TB (tuberculosis) test for every patient.

According to economist Mariana Professor Mazzucato, the concept of "value creation" involves producing useful things, while "value extraction" is simply the act of moving around existing resources and benefiting from that activity. In health care, managing the value creators, such as nurses, doctors, pharmacists, and clinical activity teams, can result in value extraction by managers who hinder the flow and contribute to waste.

Critical thinking and judgment are essential skills for nurses and doctors to make sound decisions, but the value of such decision-making is often undervalued. Electronic medical records and evidence-based medicine protocols should not be a substitute for the value of decision-making based on experience and common sense. The value of having a well-equipped hospital staffed with a CT tech is clear, but the salaries of the executive suite should also be scrutinized to determine if they are value creators or value extractors.

Karl Marx's concept of surplus value extraction is an apt analogy for executives who may not be contributing to the value creation of the hospital but are extracting value from the work of ED staff. Thus, health care organizations must reexamine their value evaluation processes to ensure that they account for the contributions of those who provide care and decision-making expertise.

In order to revitalize health care, it is crucial to examine the aforementioned components in depth. This will enable us to allocate resources effectively toward technologies that truly enhance the value of health care, rather than relying solely on the EMR. By measuring value extraction, we can streamline organizational structures that hinder progress and growth and work toward reducing inequality by improving access, quality, and cost.

## Value-Based Health Care: A Critical Examination

A number of semantic gimmicks arose out of Obamacare as a proxy for reform. One such program is "value-based health care." As we have established how difficult it is to define value when there are so many components of the patient care process, such as patients, care-givers, health insurance, government, etc., etc. With its promise of decreasing the cost of health care, Obamacare and its focus on value is fantasy. By relying on yet another definition of value by "political" economists who crafted the bill, Obamacare in a sense is nothing more than another demonstration of sophism.

Relying on value as the means of controlling costs and improving quality of care is far too simplistic and actually insulting to the professionalism of nurses and physicians who provide patient care. We aim to provide value to every patient's quest for health. If a cookbook called "value based health care" is the best we can take out of a 906 page piece of legislator, then the American public has been seriously short changed.

Deploying the semantics of persuasion (Bentham, *The Handbook of Political Fallacies*, 1824), Congress near the stroke of midnight pushed through Obamacare with this faulty attempts of reform.

Absent from Obamacare is any mention of reforming one of the major costs of health care, so-called defensive medicine.

Doctors and hospitals function under the constant cloud of being sued for medical errors for either omission or commission.

Defensive medicine, equates to ordering duplicative tests to ward off being sued by plaintiffs' attorneys. There is nothing in Obamacare to address these costs, and it is a fallacy.

Due to the input from inventory government programs that finance and regulate health care, i.e., Medicare, Medicaid, Obamacare, VA, health care, TriCor, etc., we find health care very much intersecting with politics.

Henry Hazlitt, business journalist, summed up that "the main problem we face today is not economic, but political," and that is in part due to "overlooking secondary consequences" (*Economics in One Lesson*, 1968).

Imposing political concepts of value on patient care is the biggest dilemma to producing any quality of health care.

# Chapter Twenty-Seven

# Calling On All "Doctors of Humanity"

*"There's no such thing as a free lunch."*
—*Milton Friedman*

*"The times call for courage. The times call for hard work. But if the demands are high, it is because the stakes are even higher … The future of civilization."*
—*Henry Hazlitt*

The Russian invasion of Ukraine has cast an additional pall on top of the recent existential threat of the Covid-19 pandemic. Can the United States sustain supplying both "guns" to Ukraine and the "batter" of social programs such as social security and health care?

How will economists help in meeting these challenges of supply and demand?

In his 2021 book, *Economic Truths: There's No Free Lunch*, David Bahnsen masterfully elucidates the role of economics in addressing the delicate balance between finite supply and infinite demand, critical to promote human flourishing.

While politicians constantly promote addition of more services to government-funded health programs, it's left to doctors of all persuasions to meet this demand. We need help desperately! Bahnsen's conception of economics shares a common purpose with medicine, namely the advancement of human well-being.

As economists participate in the convergence of politics and business interests that has helped to create the grossly unequal distribution of access to safe and high-quality health care services in the United States, can they join forces with practitioners of patient care to remedy this imbalance?

## "Doctors of Humanity"

Some economists humbly (ha ha) describe themselves as "doctors of humanity."

Can economists play a role in saving the health care patient?

In 1890, the esteemed Professor Alfred Marshall of Cambridge University published *Principles in Economics*, the first economic book since Adam Smith's *Health of a Nation* (1776). Marshall declared that economics is a study of the ordinary business of life, as it pertains to mankind.

Since then, the study of economics, as it pertains to health care in particular, has become exceedingly complex.

Health care services require vast sums of money that consume more and more of governmental budget outlays of developed countries. These macroeconomic-sized, eye-catching numbers dominate the attention of economists who specialize in health care. However, it's the billions of decisions at the point of care, microeconomics if you will, that go into the creation of the enormous demands.

These interactions all have the common factor of decision-making involving every aspect of the process.

Problem-solving and decision-making determine value, quality, safety, and efficiency at the point of service and their consequent cost.

Problem-solving and decision-making are driven in part by incentives, biased language, and other aspects of intelligence.

The opportunity for both optimizing value and controlling costs resides within the microeconomics of the patient encounter. Some of these categories are listed in Table 3.

## Table 3: Economic Targets for Optimizing Decision-Making in Patient Care

**Government Mandates:**
**Medicare/Medicaid—Obamacare (Politicians)**

- Commercial health insurance
- Health care delivery organizations
- Patients (moral hazard, risk, knowledge "consumerism")
- Provider (professionalism, ethics)

- Training of health care professionals
- Economic "fruits" and "sins"

The optimal approach to saving health care would involve a hybrid model, pairing economists with humanitarians in order to create more valuable models of decision-making in patient care.

It would involve application of the principles of "humanomics," the humanistic science of economics.

In *Bettering Humanomics: A New, and Old, Approach to Economic Science* (2021), Professor Deirdre Nansen McCloskey makes the case for the revival and re-infusion of the spirit of Adam Smith and the humanities into economics.[51]

The ability to get across knowledge in a way that instills confidence and commitment to an optimal course of diagnosis and treatment is the greatest opportunity for value.

---

51  This is what economist Alfred Marshall referred to as "the ordinary business of life" in his 1890 textbook *Principles of Economics*.

## Chapter Twenty-Eight

# The Dysfunctional Health Care Market

The Covid-19 pandemic, while undoubtedly tragic, presents an unprecedented opportunity for "creative destruction" of health care in the United States and around the world. This wake-up call, the "mother of all wake-up calls" for Western society, has illuminated the status of efforts for meaningful progress in reducing inequality in access to basic, safe, and high-quality health services in the United States.

The question is not whether the United States in particular spends too much on health care, it's how and why so much is wasted and what to do about it. The pandemic has shone a bright light on the discrepancy between perception and reality, highlighting the persistent inequality that manifested during the pandemic by higher morbidity and mortality amongst the poor and aged.

This disparity is a pivotal moment for acting on discussions about health care reform that fill political echo chambers, perpetuating the same old rhetoric and reverence for the status quo and stifling progress. This is a moment of opportunity for creative destruction of the forces holding health care reform hostage to its economic masters.

**We must recognize that:**

The "market" economics of health care in the United States is a "market for lemons," producing the inequality of access, quality, safety, and efficiency of health services.

This dysfunctional health care market has many ineffective and sometimes corrupt parts. Let's start with its management.

The "Golden Age of American Management" referred to in the book *The Puritan Gift* took place in the 1920–1970 period and is history literally! Present lay health care delivery organizations (i.e., hospitals) maintain ossified fortresses of bureaucracy that shield archaic management hierarchies from accountability for their decisions.

Health care markets are akin to the same kind of markets that neoclassical economics defined in the early 1900s. Neoclassical economics, based on supply and demand as the lever for "production and consumption of goods and services," is subject to manipulation by the executives and managers of organizational hierarchies whose self-interest is inextinguishable. Health care delivery is now almost entirely led and managed by administrators who use a playbook that is taken from business schools disconnected from the humanitarian mission of healing the sick.

Management and leadership in health care organizations are focused on maintaining their systems' equilibrium as a pre-pandemic status quo over all other considerations.

In classical economics, this group of individuals is referred to as "rent seekers" because they control the means of production and derive profit from those who need to use those means for their work. The surplus value these workers create is the "rent" that executives extract from their labors.

For hospitals, control over the facilities (beds, operating rooms) and staff (nurses, techs) necessary for surgeons to perform operations and inpatient services reinforces the power and control of the hospital executives.

The "rent-seeking" by hospitals through control of these critical delivery components reinforces a parallel universe with a culture of power without accountability of the executives or those directly responsible for patient care.

In health care, the management and executives act as the bourgeoisie, manipulating the proletariat (nurses/doctors) within hospitals. This is outlined in Karl Marx's *Communist Manifesto* (1848) as the reality of class struggle. This situation of cultural divergence for patient care in hospitals creates competition for resources between hospital management, which is cost-focused, and nurses and doctors, who are patient care focused.

For the United States, the government's financing through Medicare/Medicaid/Obamacare, etc. reinforces the dysfunctional health care market that fails to have accountability for producing adequate access to safe, high-quality health care.

The creative destruction of the myths of adequacy of health care delivery is a mixed blessing of the pandemic.

The dysfunctional health care marketing of the United States, with its erroneous priorities, is ripe for innovation. Will government and business interests allow for innovation in health care?

The current state of affairs is no longer viable for hedgehogs, like in the story of the "Hedgehog and the Fox" by Isaiah Berlin, who cling to one idea or model. It's time to start making lemonade out of lemons.

# Chapter Twenty-Nine

## It's Crunch Time for Health Care

*"These are the times in which a genius would wish to live. Great necessities call out great virtues."*
—Abigail Adams (1744–1818), wife of President John Adams and mother of John Q. Adams, President of the United States

The frontline nurses, doctors, and their teams who have faced the overwhelming challenges of the Covid-19 pandemic, relied upon grit, self-resilience, and professionalism. These health professionals possessed tenacity and humanity combined with unwavering dedication. Can they survive the aftereffects of the pandemic, which produced burnout and consequent exit of many, with their irreplaceable skills, experience, and humanity? This is the reality of post-pandemic health care.

The professional staff have borne the brunt of the stress of caring for stricken patients while the administrators and executives of health care delivery systems remain unscathed. Like zombies, they carried on, supporting their organizational cultures and hierarchical business structures with conformity and groupthink (William H. Whyte). Groupthink is a state of mind that is as deadly to innovative thinking as the Covid-19 virus was at its peak.

Without innovation, health care organizations of all stripes will fail to learn from their failures during the pandemic.

One striking example of this was the globalization of the supply chain for masks, gowns, and gloves. During the pandemic, severe disruptions of the global supply chain for these basic but critical items occurred. Patient care support involves more than spreadsheets.

The Covid-19 pandemic was an event of "creative destruction" (Schumpeter) of our expensive and fragmented health care systems. To improve health care, we must all accept the reality of a system that had, aside from the efforts of heroic health care workers, fallen so short.

Innovation at all levels of health care, including policy, finance, and delivery, must be allowed to occur despite the history of zombie health care management.

## Chapter Thirty

## The "Unended" Quest

*"The difficulty lies not so much in developing new ideas as in escaping from the old ones."*

—Keynes

As Admiral Stockdale, the longest-held POW of the Vietnam War, once said about his strategy for survival, it is crucial to maintain faith in one's eventual triumph while also confronting the harsh realities of the present. In the realm of health care provision and service delivery, particularly in the aftermath of Covid, such a reality involves recognizing the ongoing inequality of access to safe, high-quality, and efficient patient care services.

Despite the highest degree of per-capita funding in the world, the health care–industrial complex of the United States continues to fall short of fulfilling this obligation. The obstacle lies in the mismanagement of the process that authorizes the finances for allocation of resources, compounded by an uneven quality of delivery of patient care resources.

At the heart of this process lies the need for better decision-making. It is incumbent upon all stakeholders to assume accountability with recognition that humanism above all is a vital factor in counteracting the competing demands of business control of health care.

The mission of nursing and medicine is an "unending quest."[52] However, this mission must not be controlled, distorted, or corrupted by political or business interests, lest we risk a total collapse of patient care. Every encounter with a suffering individual should transcend self-interest. As privileged helpers, we must support this quest.

The majority of our efforts should be invested in this unending quest, and the tools of innovation should not be subverted by business interests.

The tyranny of dead ideas that dominate health care delivery organizations and public policy to bring about creative disruption of patient care was unleashed by the pandemic. Only through such disruption can we overcome the obstacles posed by the health care–industrial complex and renew our commitment to the equity of patient care.

---

52   Popper, Karl. *Unended Quest: An Intellectual Autobiography.* Open Court Publishing Company, 1976.

# Conclusion

*"God grant me the courage not to give up what I think is right even though I think it is hopeless."*

—Admiral Chester Nimitz
Commander, Pacific Ocean Theater of War
World War II

Perversely, the power over our health care resides not with us but with politicians and their massive governmental bureaucracies and agencies, and it is controlled either directly by business interests or indirectly by those trained in business management.

The actual "care," still in the hands of those trained in the healing arts (for now), is in competition with these political/business forces.

I wrote this book based upon the amazing privilege I've had to improve the lives of people and the good fortune also to be able to do it for a long time. As such, I have the perspective along with the experience to see where patient care is going.

The trend is not good.

Taking care of patients has become a big business, and consequently most of the people in the business of health care don't help to take care of people. Actually, they divert valuable resources from patient care and create more problems with patient care than they help solve, and they profit from the misfortune of others as well.

I'd like to think, like Dilma Rousseff (impeached president of Brazil, 2016), that while "reality has changed and we changed with it ... I have never changed sides. I have always been on the side of justice, democracy and social equality."

Furthermore, at the risk of seeming more of an unrepentant scold, I have followed Ms. Rousseff's spirit in bringing the harsh light of day on the tenuous state of health care and the reasons for it. "Do not expect from me the obsequious silence of cowards."

There's no sugarcoating for the arrogance and self-interest that dominates health care.

Can we manage to save health care?

Only if we admit that patient care is on the wrong track due to erroneous public policy, misguided management, feckless leadership, and outright greed.

The tragedy of the pandemic should be a reminder of the state of this self-imposed decay at the heart of our health care institutions. There is always an opportunity to boldly face these limitations and prepare for future challenges of access to safe, high-quality health services.

Those of us who have dedicated ourselves to the essence of patient care must maintain the strength of that conviction and summon the courage to reverse the tide.

As writer Aleksandr Solzhenitsyn, no stranger to trial and tribulation, said, "I am only a sword made sharp to smite the unclean forces. An enchanted sword to cleave and disperse them. Grant, O Lord, that I may not break as I strike. Let me not fall from thy hand !"

Spero contra spem! (I hope against hope!)

# About the Author

Pictured with George is a portrait of Paul Bucy, M.D. former Chairman of Neurosurgery. Dr Bucy was a pioneer in the field and a great gentleman.

George Cybulski has devoted most of his life to the medical care of people (and his pet friends). This book was written on the basis of over 40 years as a doctor and 35 years as a Neurosurgeon. This book offers a diagnosis and suggestion of a treatment plan for the structured ills that impact the ability to uniformly provide equitable medical care.

George received his M.D. from the University of Illinois College of Medicine, where he had wonderful mentors who served as an example to follow of humanistic ideals of medicine.

After many years of patient care, an M.B.A. in Health Care Management from Loyola University, Chicago enabled George to perform a dissection of the aspects of health care—the big business that patient care has become in order to "manage" to save health care.

The business of health care almost collapsed during the Covid Pandemic, and this warning must not be ignored.

Far from appearances, health care remains in perilous condition.

# Bibliography

## Bibliographical Appendix

I have grouped my reference section into categories based on an assessment of value to the process of understanding, sourcing, and demonstrating the intersection of the healing arts of medicine and business take-over. I have created categories of references, therefore, based on the concept of utility (not strictly in an economic sense, however, pun intended).

The "Essential" references I have found most worthwhile both in terms of enlightenment and actual enjoyment. The "Academic" references are for those sticklers (and you know who you are) who require a reference for everything. The "Optional" references exist for citation but not recommendation—basically, I have read them so you don't have to.

A customary disclaimer: The practice of medicine, the literature of business management, philosophy and economics (political philosophy), and the exhaustive literature of these subjects are all critical to understanding the dilemma and solution for saving health care. Therefore, no single reference can possibly address all of the foibles of human nature that have contributed to the challenge of patient care.

If anything, hopefully my effort moves you. Please keep digging for the truth about what we all should be getting for ourselves and our families. As the French mathematician and physicist Blaise Pascal said, "Keep looking for the truth, it wants to be found."

## Essential References

These are the most worthwhile books and articles of the foibles of human nature, its myths of achievement through management organization, and its effects on health care—directly and indirectly.

Aaron, Henry J.: *Serious and Unstable Condition: Financing America's Healthcare* —Brookings Institute Press, Washington D.C., 1991 (Author Cybulski's Note: I met the great man when I was in my prime as a neurosurgeon, a long time before I realized that the game was up. I'm glad I didn't read his book in 1991, or I may have fallen on my scalpel.)

Adashi, Eli; O'Mahoney, Daniel P.; Cohen, I. Glen: "The Affordable Care Act Resurrected: Curtailing the Ranks of the Uninsured" —*JAMA Network* JAMA, 2021, 326(18): 1797–1798, doi:10.1001/jama.2021.17531

Alchian, Armen A.; Woodward, Susan: "The Firm is Dead; Long Live The Firm: A Review of Oliver E. Williamson's 'The Economic Institutions of Capitalism'" in *The Collected Works of Armen A. Alchian. Vol. 2* —Liberty Fund Inc., Indianapolis, 321–345, 2006

Argyris, Chris: *Organizational Traps. Leadership, Culture, Organizational Design* —Oxford University Press; NY 2010

Bagehot: "Labor is Right—Karl Marx Has A Lot to Teach Today's Politicians" —*The Economist*, May 11, 2017, http://www.economist.com/news/britain/21721916-shadoco-chancellors-comment-provoked-scorn-yet-marx-becomes-more-relevant-day-labour?

Bahnsen, David L.: *There's No Free Lunch: 250 Economic Truths* —Post Hill Press, New York, NY, 2021

Bastiat, Frederic (General) Editor Jacques de Guenin: *Economic Sophisms and "What is Seen and What is Not Seen" The Collected Works of Frederic Bastiat 3*, —Liberty Fund, Inc., 2016

Berlin, Isaiah: *The Hedgehog and the Fox. An Essay on Tolstoy's View of History* —Ivan R Dee, Publisher, Chicago, IL, 1993

Bernstein, Peter L.: *Against the Gods: The Remarkable Story of Risk* —John Wiley and Sons, Inc., New York, 1996

Bloomfield, Daniel K.: *Keys to the Asylum: A Dean, a Medical School, and Academic Politics* —New Medical Press, Champaign, IL, 2000 (Author Cybulski's Note: I had the fortune to have this great man as my first dean in medical school. Over forty years later, I have not encountered the likes of him. He was a rare servant leader in medical education.)

Brammer, Stephen; Branick, Layla; Linnenluecke, Martina K.: "Covid-19, Societalization and the Future of Business in Society" —*Academy of Management Perspectives,* 34(4): 493–507, 2020

Bregman, Rutger; et al: *Humankind: A Hopeful History* — Little, Brown & Company, New York, 2020

Campbell, Joseph, et al: *The Hero with a Thousand Faces* —New World Library, Novato, CA, 3rd Edition, 2008

Carse, James P.: *The Finite and Infinite Games: A Vision of Life as Play and Possibility* —Free Press, New York, 1986

Chandler, Alfred D. Jr.: *The Visible Hand: The Managerial Revolution in American Business* —Belknap Press of Harvard University Press; Cambridge, MA, 1977, 16th printing, 2002

Clough, David R.; Wu, Andy: "Artificial Intelligence, Data-Driven Learning and the Decentralized Structure of Platform Ecosystems" —*Academy of Management Review* 47 (1):184–192, 2022. (Author Cybulski's Note: The idea for deploying technology for unlocking value—this is essential for the Holy Grail of true value in health care reform.)

Coase, Ronald, H.: *The Firm, the Market and the Law* —University of Chicago Press, 1988

Cohn, Amanda C.; Mahon, Barbara E.; Walensky, Rochelle P.: "One Year of Covid-19 Vaccines: A Shot of Hope, a Dose of Reality"—*JAMA Network*, 2022, JAMA, 2022, 327(2): 119–120, doi:10.1001/jama.2021.23962

Coiera, Enrico: "Why System Inertia Makes Health Reform So Difficult" —*BMJ*, 343: 27–29, 2011 (accessed 8/19/2015)

Coyle, Diane: *Cogs and Monsters: What Economic Is, and What It Should Be* —Princeton University Press, Princeton and Oxford, NJ, 2021

Dafny, Leemore S.: "Does CVS-Aetna Spell the End of Business as Usual?" —*The New England Journal of Medicine*, 387(7): 593–595, 2018

Deaton, Angus: *The Great Escape. Health, Wealth and the Origins of Inequality* —Princeton University Press, NJ, 2013

Denning, Steve: "How Not to Fix U.S. Healthcare: Copy the Cheesecake Factory" —*Forbes,* August 13, 2021 (accessed 2/7/2022)

Deresiewicz, William: *Excellent Sheep: The Miseducation of the American Elite and the Way to a Meaningful Life* —Free Press, New York, 2014 (Author Cybulski's note: The title of this book captures for me the type of doctor in medical schools who, with rare exception, give up their hard-earned privilege to treat patients for the bureaucracy and games of academic medicine.)

Dorfman, Daniel I.: "Pandemic a factor as Lake Forest Hospital officials start expansion process; 'The volume of patients (shows) ... we need to plan for the next phase of evolution'" —*Chicago Tribune,* January 29, 2002

*Economics of Uncertainty* —Books LLC, Wiki Series, Memphis, USA, 2011

Feldstein, Martin (Forward); Bucholz Todd G.: *New Ideas from Dead Economists* —Plume Printing, 1990

Feynman, Richard P.; Ralph Leighton: *Surely You're Joking, Mr. Feynman! (Adventures of a Curious Character)* —W.W. Norton & Co., New York, 1997

Freedman, Sir Lawrence: *Strategy: A History* —Oxford University Press, Oxford, 2013 (Author Cybulski's note: An incredible comprehensive repository of all of the aspects that have gone into formulating strategy in all of humankind's arenas of endeavor.)

Frigo, Mark L.; Litman, Joel: *Driven: Business Strategy Human Actions, and the Creation of Wealth* —Strategy & Execution LLC, 2007

Gaddis, John L.: *The Landscape of History* —Oxford University Press, New York, 2002

Gaddis, John L.: *On Great Strategy* —Penguin Press, New York, 2018

Gardner, Howard: *Changing Minds: The Art and Science of Changing Our Own and Other People's Minds* —Harvard Business School Publishing, Boston, 2006

Gherson, Diane; Grafton, Lynda: "Managers Can't Do It All: It's Time to Reinvent Their Role for the New World of Work" —*Harvard Business Review*, March–April 2022

Gigerenzer, Gerd: *Risk Savvy: How to Make Good Decisions* —Penguin Books, New York, 2014

Gollust, Sarah; Lynch, Julia (Special Issue Editors): "Covid-19 Politics and Policy: Pandemic Inequity in the United States" —*Journal of Health Politics, Policy and Law*, Vol. 46, No. 5, October 2021

Gostin, Lawrence O.: "The Coronavirus Pandemic 1 Year On—What Went Wrong?" —*The Journal of the American Medical Association*, Vol. 325, No. 12, 1132–1133, 2021, Georgetown Law Faculty Publications and Other Works, doi:10.1001/jama.2021.3207

Graeber, David: *Bullshit Jobs: A Theory* —Simon and Schuster, New York, 2018

Gray, Colin S.: *The Future of Strategy* —Polity Press, Cambridge, 2015

Grogan, Collene M.; Lin, Yu An; Gusmano, Michael K.: "Unsanitized and Unfair: How Covid-19 Bailout Funds Refuel Inequity in the U.S. Health Care System" —*Journal of Health Politics, Policy and Law*, 46(5): 785–809, 2021

Hammer, Peter J.; Haas-Wilson, Deborah; Peterson, Mark A.; Sage, William M. (editors): *Uncertain Times: Kenneth Arrow and the Changing Economics of Health Care.* —Duke University Press, Durham and London, 2003

Handy, Charles: *Gods of Management:The Changing Work of Organizations* —Oxford University Press, New York and Oxford 1996

Hardin, Garrett: "The Tragedy of the Commons" —*Science New Series*, Vol. 162, No.3859, 1243–1248, 1968, American Association for the Advancement of Science

Hartzband, Pamela; Groopman, Jerome: "Money and the Changing Culture of Medicine" —*The New England Journal of Medicine,* 360(2): 101–103, 2009

Hazlitt, Henry: *Economics in One Lesson: The Shortest and Surest Way to Understand Basic Economics* —Three Rivers Press, New York, 1979

Hill, Andrew: *Financial Times*—The Big Read, "US Business" June 30/July 1, 2018 (accessed 2018)

Hoff, Timothy J.: *Next in Line: Lowered Care Expectations in the Age of Retail and Value-Based Health* —Oxford University Press, New York, 2018

Hoffman, Pauil B. (edited); Perry, Frankie (front matter): *Management Mistakes in Healthcare: Identification, Correction, and Prevention* —Cambridge University Press, UK, 2005 (Author Cybulski's Note: A Rare Discussion of the Foibles of Healthcare Management.)

Hoopes, James: *False Prophets: The Gurus Who Created Modern Management and Why Their Ideas Are Bad for Business Today* —Perseus Book Group, Cambridge, MA, 2003

Hopper, Kenneth and Hopper, William: *The Puritan Gift: Reclaiming the American Dream Amidst Global Financial Chaos* —IB Tauris 2009, London, 2009

Hubbard, Al; Blase, Brian: "High-Priced Hospitals in Indiana Press Their Political Luck" —*The Wall Street Journal*, Feb 4, 2022

Hurst, David: *The New Ecology of Leadership: Business Mastery in a Chaotic World* —Columbia Business School Publishing, NY, 2012

Illich, Ivan: *Medical Nemesis: The Expropriation of Health* —Panthenon, 1982

Jenkins, Holman W. Jr.: "Obamacare is Popular Because it Failed" —*The Wall Street Journal* (accessed 4/28/2019)

Jenkins, Holman W. Jr.: "A Workaholic Saved Chrysler" —*The Wall Street Journal*, July 25, 2018, page A17 (accessed 7/26/2018)

Johnson-Laird, PN: "The History of Mental Models" —PDF, http://mentalmoderls.princetonedu/papers/2005 (accessed 2/14/2022)

Kadakia, Kushal T.; Howell, Michael D.; DeSalvo, Karen B.: Viewpoint: "Modernizing Public Health Data Systems, Lessons from the Health Information Technology for Economic and Clinical Health (HITECH) Act" —*JAMA Network 2021*, JAMA. 2021, 326(5): 385–386, doi:10.1001/jama.2021.12000 (Author Cybulski's Note: This with a former federal health apprentice commentary comes right up to the line of stating the obvious, that the federally funded imposition of EMRs mainly achieved through an overly broad mandate of "meaningful use" accomplished an exercise in compliance rather than an evolution in system capabilities.)

Kay, John; King, Mervyn: *Radical Uncertainty: Decision Making Beyond the Number.* —W.W. Norton & Company, New York, 2020

Khara, Rakesh: *From Higher Aims to Hired Hands: The Social Transformation of American Business Schools and the Unfulfilled Promise of Mangement as a Profession* —Princeton University Press, 2007

Kissick, William L.: *Medicine's Dilemmas: Infinite Needs vs Finite Resources* —Yale University Press; New Haven and London, 1994

Klein, Gary A: *Sources of Power: How People Make Decisions* —*The MIT Press*, Cambridge, MA, 1999 (Author Cybulski's Note: The basis of "good power" for making better decisions.)

Krugman, Paul: *Arguing With Zombies: Economics, Politics, and the Fight for a Better Future* W.W. Norton & Company, New York, 2020

Lee, Thomas H.; Cosgrove, Toby: "Engaging Doctors in the Health Care Revolution" —*Harvard Business Review*, 105–111, June 2014 (George R. Cybulski Letter to Editor – Response to Article, October 2014)

LeGrand, Julian (2007) wrote about the prominence of *The Other Invisible Hand: Delivering Public Services through Choice and Competition* —Princeton University Press, 2007

Lewis, Harry: *Excellence Without Soul: How a Great University Forgot Education* —Public Affairs, New York, 2006

Lindsey, Brink and Teles, Steven M.: *The Captured Economy: How the Powerful Enrich Themselves, Slow Down Growth, and Increase Inequity* —Oxford University Press, 2017

Lockwood, David: *Fooled by the Winners: How Survivor Bias Deceives Us* —Greenleaf Book Group Press, 2021

McGraw, Thomas K.: *Prophet of Innovation: Joseph Schumpeter and Creative Destruction* —The Belkmap Press of Harvard University Press, 2007

McNeill, William H.: *Plagues and Peoples* —Doubleday, 1976

Machiavelli, Niccolo: *The Prince and Other Writings* —Barnes and Noble Classics, New York, 2003; (Author Cybulski's Note: Originally published as *Il principe* (The Prince) in 1513, while he was incarcerated. This remains the classic playbook for the blackguards who occupy industrial health care today.)

Madden, Bartley J.: *Value Creation Principles: The Pragmatic Theory of the Firm That Begins with Purpose and Ends with Sustainable Capitalism* —John Wiley and Sons, 2020

Malraux, Andre: *Man's Fate (Le Condition Humaine)* — Random House, Reissue 1990

Marx, Karl: *Capital: A Critique of Political Economy, Volume 1:* —Penguin Classic Services, Reprint 1992

Miller, Matt: *The Tyranny of Dead Ideas: Letting Go of the Old Ways of Thinking to Unleash a New Prosperity* —Times Books, Henry Holt & Company; New York, 2009

Mitroff, Ian I: *Dumb, Deranged, and Dangers: A Smart Guide to Combating Dumb Arguments* —Self-published, 2015

Mitzberg, Henry: *Manger Not MBAs: A Hard Look at the Soft Practice of Managing and Management Development* —Berrett-Koehler Publishers, 2005

Mitzberg, Henry: *Managing* —Berrett-Koehler Publishers, 2011

Mitzberg, Henry: *Managing the Myths of Healthcare: Bridging the Separations between Care, Cure, Control, and Community* —Berrett-Koehler Publishers, 2017

Moazed, Alex; Johnson, Nicholas L.: *Modern Monopolies: What It Takes to Dominate the 21st Century Economy* — St. Martin's Press, 2016

Morris, Thomas V.: *Making Sense of It All: Pascal and the Meaning of Life* —William B. Eerdmans Publishing Company, Grand Rapids, MI, 1992 (Author Cybulski's Note: A book astounding for its erudition and inspiration sharing the work of the mathematician-philosopher Blaise Pascal.)

Morson, Gary S.; Schapiro, Morton: *Cents and Sensibility: What Economics Can Learn From the Humanities* —Princeton University Press, 2017

McCloskey, Deirdre N.: *Bettering Humanomics: A New, and Old, Approach to Economic Science* —University of Chicago Press, 2021

Nasar Sylvia: *Grand Pursuit: The Story of Economic Genius* —Simon and Schuster, 2011

Otteson, James R.: *Seven Deadly Economic Sins; Obstacles to Prosperity and Happiness Every Citizen Should Know* — Cambridge University Press, 2021

Peshwaria, Rajeev: *Too Many Bosses, Too Few Leaders: The Three Essential Principles You Need to Become an Extraordinary Leader* —Free Press, 2011

Popper, Karl: *Unended Quest: An Intellectual Autobiography* —Open Court Publishing Company, 1976. (Author Cybulski's Note: Pure distilled wisdom for the "unended quest" to save health care.)

Porter, Roy: *The Greatest Benefit to Mankind* —W.W. Norton and Company, 1997

Porter, Michael E.: "What is Value in Healthcare?" —*New England Journal of Medicine*, 2010

Rein, Richard K: *American Urbanist: How William H. Whyte's Unconventional Wisdom Reshaped Public Life* —Island Press, 2022

Rosenzweig, Phil: *The Halo Effect and the Eight Other Business Delusions That Deceive Managers* —Free Press, 2007

Province, Charles M.: *Patton's One-Minute Messages: Tactical Leadership Skills for Business Managers* —Ballantine Books, 1995 (Author Cybulski's Note: Strategic and tactical principles that are inspirational for obtaining greater achievement are timeless. This fantastic compendium reminds us of this fact.)

Rosovsky, Henry: *The University: An Owner's Manuel* W.W. Norton, 1990, pg. 259

Sandel, Michael J.: *What Money Can't Buy: The Moral Limits of Markets* —Penguin Books, 2013

Sapolsky, Robert M.: *Behave: The Biology of Humans at Our Best and Worst* —Penguin Press, 2017

Scandlen, Greg: *Myth Busters: Why Health Reform Always Goes Awry* —Self-published, 2017

Schelling, Thomas C.: *Micromotives and Macrobehavior* —W. W. Norton & Company, 2006

Schrager Allison: An Economist Walks into a Brothel: And Other Unexpected Places to Understand Risk —Penguin Press, 2019

Schumpeter, Joseph: "The Three Habits of Highly Irritating Management Gurus" —*The Economist*, October 24, 2009

Soros, George: "Fallibility, Reflexivity, and the Human Uncertainty Principle" —*Journal of Economic Methodology,* January 2014 (Author Cybulski's Note: An exceptional presentation of the position of uncertainty in economic decision making from an individual with a controversial role in the recent history of economic markets.)

Sowell, Thomas: *Economic Facts and Fallacies* —Basic Books, 2008

Sowell, Thomas: *Applied Economics* —Basic Books, 2009

Stern, Stefan: *How to Be a Better Leader* —Bluebird, 2019

Sutton, Robert I.: *The No Asshole Rule: Building a Civilized Workplace and Surviving One That Isn't* —Business Plus, 2010; Hachette Book Group, 2007

Thornhill, John: "Covid-19 Will Change Healthcare Forever" —*Financial Times*, December 18, 2020

Tourish, Dennis: *The Dark Side of Transformational Leadership: A Critical Perspective* —Routledge, 2013

Tourish, Dennis: *Management Studies in Crisis: Fraud, Deception, and Meaningless Research* —Cambridge University Press, 2019

Varol, Ozan: *Think Like a Rocket Scientist: Simple Strategies You Can Use to Make Giant Leaps in Work and Life,* —Public Affairs, 2020

Wapshott, Nicholas: *Samuelson Friedman: The battle Over the Free Market* —W.W. Norton & Company, 2021

Weinzimmer, Lawrence G.; McConoughey, Jim: *The Wisdom of Failure: How to Learn the Tough Leadership Lessons Without Paying the Price* —Jossey-Bass, 2013

Westfall, Chris: "Leadership Development Is a $366 Billion Industry: Here's Why Most Programs Don't Work" —*Forbes* (accessed 6/19/2019)

Wilensky, Gail R.: "2020 Revealed How Poorly the US was Prepared for Covid-19 and Future Pandemics" —*Journal of the American Medical Association*, 325(11): 1029–1030

Zak, Paul J.: "The Neuroscience of Trust" —*Harvard Business Review*, Jan–Feb 2017, 84–90

## Further Reading of Interest

I read these so you don't have to, i.e., from the ponderous to the "classics," to the hyped beyond measure, and tomes written by legends in their own minds for other legends in their own minds.

Kahneman, Daniel: *Thinking Fast and Slow* —Farrar, Straus and Giroux, 2013 (Author Cybulski's Note: Emphasis on the slow-going; quite a doorstopper of a book.)

Babiak Paul; Hare Robert D.: *Snakes in Suits: When Psychopaths Go To Work* —HarperCollins Business, 2007

Battilana, Julie; Casciaro, Tiziana: *Power for All: How It Really Works and Why It's Everyone's Business* —Simon & Schuster, New York, 2021 (Author Cybulski's Note: A complete waste of time as the analysis is superficial and unenlightening. Amazed that it was even published.)

Bucheron, Patrick: *Machiavelli: The Art of Teaching People What to Fear* (Translated from the French by Willard Wood) —Other Press, New York, 2017

Burkner, Hans-Paul; Bhattacharya, Arindam: "Squaring the Circle: Leading Companies in a Contradicting World" —*BCG Henderson Institute*, 2020 (accessed 12/7/21)

Chang Huan J.; Liang, Matthew H.: "A Piece of My Mind: The Quiet Epidemic" —*Journal of the American Medical Association*, 306: 1843–44, 2011

Christensen, Clayton M.: *The Innovator's Dilemma: The Revolutionary Book That Will Change the Way You Do Business* —Harper Paperbacks, 1997 (Author Cybulski's note: Still waiting for such a book.)

Collins, Jim: *Good to Great* —HarperCollins, New York, 2001 (Author Cybulski's Note: One of the "classics" about successful businesses, but not many health care organizations here.)

Cybulski, George, R.: "Letter to the Editor: Response to 'Engaging Doctors in the Health Care Revolution' by TH Lee and T Cosgrove" —*Harvard Business Review,* June 2014; Response Published October 2014

Gawande, Atul: "Big Med" —*The New Yorker,* August 6, 2021 (accessed 11/17/21 and 2/7/2022) (Author Cybulski's Note: As an example, the suggestion of Boston surgeon and *New Yorker* writer Atul Gawande suggests in his article "Big Med" that the national chain restaurant, The Cheesecake Factory, is a model for the kind of standardization and quality that have been lacking in health care. He argues that their model for delivering "delicious meals" represents the kind of affordable, reliable product that would better fit the budgets of cost-conscious health care while meeting the needs of their *customers*–in the competitive new world of medicine.)

Graban, Mark: *Lean Hospitals* —Productivity Press, New York, 2009 (Author Cybulski's Note: Hospitals require "kaikaku," Japanese for "radical or transformational change.")

Joullie, Jean-Etienne; Gould, Anthony M.: "Having Nothing to Say But Saying It Anyway: Language and Practical Relevance in Management Research" —*Academy of Management Learning and Education*, 21(2), 2021

Harvey-Jones, John: *Making It Happen: Reflections on Leadership* —Fontana, London, 1988

Herzlinger, Regina E.: *Who Killed Health Care? America's $2 Trillion Medical Problem and the Consumer-Driven Cure* —McGraw-Hill, New York, 2007

Kacik, Alex: "C-suite pay raises target transformational and health care leaders" —*Modern Healthcare*, August 14, 2017 (accessed 2/16/2022) (Author Cybulski's Note: Leaders?? Transformational?? Where are they hiding?)

Logan, Dave; King, John; Fischer-Wright, Halee: *Tribal Leadership: Leveraging Natural Groups to Build a Thriving Organization* —HarperCollins, New York, 2008 (Author Cybulski's Note: A book dedicated to "Tribal Leaders: The Future of the Business World Depends on You." If so, we are doomed!)

MacEachern, Malcom: *Hospital Organization and Management* —Physician's Record Company, Berwyn, IL, 3rd Edition, 1962

Monk, Ray: *Ludwig Wittgenstein: The Duty of Genius* —Penguin Books USA, New York, 1990

Nundy, Shantanu; Cooper, Lisa A.; Mate, Kedar S.: "The Quintuple Aim for Health Care Improvement: A new Imperative to Advanced Health Equity" —*Journal of the American Medical Association*, 327(6): 521–22 (Author Cybulski's Note: Stating the obvious, so nothing new here!)

Mensik, Hailey: "Hospitals Request More Federal Help Battling Rising Labor Expenses, Staffing Shortages Amid Omicron" —*Healthcare Dive*, January 25, 2022

O'Donnell, Walter J.: "Reducing Administrative Harm in Medicine - Clinicians and Administrators Together" —*The New England Journal of Medicine*, 386(25): 2429–2432, 2022

Peters, Tom; Waterman Jr., Robert H.: *In Search of Excellence: Lessons from America's Best Run Companies* —Harper Business, Reprint February 7, 2006

Patashnik, Eric M.: "Introduction: Entrenchment and Health Equity" —*Journal of Health Politics, Policy and Law*, 48(2): 131–133, 2023

Pifer, Rebecca: "Cleveland Clinic reports COVID-spurred financial windfall in 2021" —*Healthcare Dive* (accessed January 31, 2022)

Porter, Michael; Teisberg, Elizabeth O.: *Redefining Health Care: Creating Value-Based Competition on Results* —Harvard Business Review Press, 2006 (Author Cybulski's Note: Dead ideas must vacate health care.)

Reinhart, Eric: "Doctors Aren't Burned Out From Overwork. We're Demoralized by Our Health System." —*The New York Times*, February 5, 2023 (accessed /02/06/2023)

Sagan, Carl: "The Fine Art of Baloney Detection" —*The Demon-Haunted World: Science as a Candle in the Dark*, Balantine Books, New York, 1996, 201–218

Sahni, Nikhil R.; Carrus, Brandon; Cutler, David M.: "Administrative Simplification and the Potential for Saving a Quarter-Trillion Dollars in Health Care" —*Journal of the American Medical Association*, 326: 1677–78, 2021

Stone, Will: "Americans get sicker as Omicron stalls everything from heart surgeries to cancer care" —*NPR*, February 4, 2022

## Academic References

Aaron, Henry J.: "The Costs of Health Care Administration in the United States and Canada – Questionable Answers to a Questionable Question" —*New England Journal of Medicine*, 349(8): 801–803, 2003

Adashi, Eli Y.; Cohen, I. G.; Elberg, Jacob T.: "Transparency and the Doctor-Patient Relationship — Rethinking Conflict-of-Interest Disclosures" —*New England Journal of Medicine*, 386(4): 300–302, 2022

Adler-Milstein, Julia; Mehotra, Ateev: "Paying for Digital Healthcare — Problems with the Fee-for-Services System" —*New England Journal of Medicine*, 385(10): 871–873, 2021

Akerlof, George: "The Market for 'Lemons': Quality, Uncertainty and the Market Mechanism" —*The Quarterly Journal of Economics*, 84(3): 488–500, 1970

Arnold-Foster, Agnes; Moses, Jacob D.; Schotland, Samuel V.: "Obstacles to Physicians' Emotional Health - Lessons from History" —*New England Journal of Medicine*, 386(1): 4–9, 2022

Arora, Vineet M.; Madison, Sonia; Simpson, Lisa: "Trust in Health Care: Addressing Medical Misinformation in the Patient Clinician Relationship" —*Journal of the American Medical Association*, 324(23): 2367–2368, 2020

Bai, Ge; Zare, Hossein; Hyman, David A.: "Evaluation of Unreimbursed Medicaid Costs Among Nonprofit and For-Profit Hospitals" —*JAMA Network Open*, 2022, 5(2) e2148232, doi:10.1001/jamanetworkopen 2021, 48232 (accessed February 2/14/2022)

Barry, John M.: "What We Can Learn From How the 1918 Pandemic Ended" —*The New York Times*, January 31, 2022 (accessed NY Times 2/6/22).

Beasley, John W.; Roberts, Richard G.; Goroll, Allan H.: "Promoting Trust and Morale by Changing How the Word Provider is Used. Encouraging specificity and Transparency" —*The Journal of the American Medical Association*, 325(23): 2343–2344, 2021

Bennett, Neil; Eggleston, Jonathan; Mykyta, Laryssa; Sullivan, Briana: "Who Had Medical Debt in the United States?" —*U.S. Census Bureau*, April 7, 2021 (accessed January 31, 2022)

Brook, Robert H.: "The Role of Physicians in Controlling Medical Care Costs and Reducing Waste" —*The Journal of the American Medical Association*, 306(6): 650–651, 2011

Bown, Chad P.; Irwin Douglas A.: "Why Does Everyone Suddenly Care About Supply Chains?" —*The New York Times*, Oct 16, 2021, A19 (accessed 10/16/2021)

Catron, David: "The Right Prescription" —*Paul Krugman's Orwellian History of Obamacare*, https://spectator.org/paul-krugmans-orwellian-history-of obamacare (accessed 6/21/2017)

Chernew, Michael; Mintz Harrison: "Administrative Expenses in the US Health Care System: Why So High?" —*The Journal of the American Medical Association*, 326(17): 1679–1680, 2021

Chernew, Michael E.: "The Role of Market Forces in U.S. Healthcare" —*The New England Journal of Medicine*, 383 (15) 1401–1404, 2021

Dafny, Leemore: "Addressing Consolidation in Health Care Markets" —*The Journal of the American Medical Association*, January 28, 2021, (accessed on 2/22/2021)

Davidson, Charles S.: "The Caring Physician: The Life of Dr. Francis Peabody" Book Review —*The New England Journal of Medicine*, 328:817–818, 1993

Vitekar, Rahul: "Peter Drucker - Why does Emergency Room in a hospital exist? Brilliant!" —*LinkedIn*, May 8, 2018

Dyrda, Laura: "Physician vs. health care CEO pay: 5 notes." —*Becker's ASC Review*, January 3, 2022 (accessed 1/3/22)

Dzau, Victor J.; Mate, Kedar; O'Kane, Margaret: "Equity and Quality – Improving Health Care Delivery Requires Both" —*The Journal of the American Medical Association*, 327(6): 519–520, 2022 (Author Cybulski's Note: No one who cares would disagree; leadership is MIA for this agenda.)

Edgecliffe-Johnson, Andrew; Kuchler, Hannah: "Leadership on the Coronavirus Frontline" —*Financial Times*, April 13, 2020 (accessed 4/14/2020)

Emannuel, Ezekiel J.; Osterholm, Michael; Gounder, Celine R.: "A National Strategy for the 'New Normal' of Life with COVID" —*The Journal of the American Medical Association*, 327(3): 211–212, 2022

Evans, Melanie; McGinty, Tom: "Hospitals Faulted on Medical-Debt Suites" —*The Wall Street Journal*, December 7, 2021 (accessed 12/7/2021)

Fiscella, Kevin; Sanders, Mechelle R.; Carroll, Jennifer K.: "Transforming Health Care to Address Value and Equity: National Vital Signs to Guide Vital Reforms" —*The Journal of the American Medical Association*, 326(2): 131–132, 2021

Fleisher, Lee A.; Schreiber, Michelle; Cardo, Denise; Srinivasan, Arjun: "Health Care Safety during the Pandemic and Beyond — Building a System That Ensures Resilience" —*The New England Journal of Medicine*, 386(7): 609–611, 2022

Galbraith, John K.: *Economics in Perspective: A Critical History* —Princeton Univerity Press, Princeton, NJ, 2017

Garber, Alan M.; Skinner, Jonathan: "Is American Health Care Uniquely Inefficient?" —*Journal of Economic Perspectives*, 22 (4): 27–50, 2008

Goldman, Devorah: "The Doctor's Office Becomes an Assembly Line" —*The Wall Street Journal*, December 30, 2021 (accessed 12/31/2021)

Goldsmith, Jeff C.: "Visions of Empire: Same problems with the corporate model of hospitals" —*Hospital Forum*, May–June 1985, 50–52

Goldstein, Joseph: "In Covid Ward: 2 Nurses Race to 36 Patients" —*The New York Times*, January 16, 2022 (accessed 1/16/22)

Graves, John A.; Baig, Khrysta; Buntin, Melinda: "The Financial Effects and Consequences of COVID-19: A Gathering Storm" —*The Journal of the American Medical Association*, 326(19): 1909–1910, 2021

Hadler, NM: Review of *Overtreated: Why Too Much Medicine Is Making Us Sicker and Poorer* by Shannon Bownlee —*The Journal of the American Medical Association*, 298(17): 2071, 2007

Hartzband, Pamela; Groopman, Jerome: "The New Language of Medicine" —*The New England Journal of Medicine*, 365: 1372–73, 2011

Herzlinger, Regina E.; Schleicher, Stephen M., Mullangi, Samyukta: "Health Care Delivery Innovations That Integrate Care? Yes!: But Integrating What?" —*The Journal of the American Medical Association*, 315(11): 1109–1110, 2016

Jin, Jill: JAMA Patient Page: "What to Consider When Reading Your Medical Notes" —*The Journal of the American Medical Association*, 326(17): 1756, 2021

Kitchener, Martin; Caronna, Carol A.; Shortell, Stephen M.: "From the doctor's workshop to the iron cage? Evolving modes of physician control in US health systems" —*Social Science and Medicine*, 60: 1311–1322, 2005

Kluender, Raymond; Mahoney, Neale; Wong, Francis; Yin, Wesley: "Medical Debt in the U.S., 2009–2020" —*The Journal of the American Medical Association*, 326(3): 250–256, 2021

Knudse, Janine; Chokshi, Dave A.: "Covid-19 and the Safety Net — Moving from Staining to Sustaining" —*The New England Journal of Medicine*, 385(24): 2209–2211, 2021

Kocher, Robert P.; Shah, Soleil; Navathe, Amol S.: "Overcoming the Market Dominance of Hospitals" —*The Journal of the American Medical Association*, 325(10): 929–30, 2021

Mendes de Leon, Carlos F.; Griggs, Jennifer J.: "Medical Debt as a Social Determinant of Health" —*The Journal of the American Medical Association*, 326(3): 228–229, 2021

Michaels, D; Emanuel, EJ; Bright, R: A National Strategy for Covid-19. Testing, Surveillance and Mitigation Strategies. —*The Journal of the American Medical Association*, 327(3): 213–214

Montgomery, Tara; Berns, Jeffrey S.; Braddock, Clarence H.: "Transparency as a Trust-Building Practice in Physician Relationships With Patients" —*The Journal of the American Medical Association*, 324(23): 2365–2366, 2020

Oakes, Allison H.; Radonski, Thomas R.: "Reducing Low-Value Care and Improving Health Care Value" —*The Journal of the American Medical Association*, 325(17): 1715–1716, 2021

Patel, Nisarg: "Hospital costs, not drug prices, are the real US health care scandal" —*Financial Times*, July 27, 2021 (accessed 7/28/2021)

Pauly, Mark V.: "The Economics of Moral Hazard: Comment" —*The American Economic Review*, 58(3): 531–537, 1968

Pauly, Mark V.: *Doctors and Their Workshops: Economic Models of Physician Behavior* —University of Chicago Press, Chicago, 1980

Physician Advocacy Institute: "Updated physician acquisition study: National and regional changes in physician employment 2012–2018" February 2019 (accessed 11/12/2021)

"Quality Programs and Medicare Promoting Interoperability Program Requirements for Eligible Hospitals and Critical Access Hospitals" —Federal Register 2021, 86(154): 45479–45483

Ranney, ML; Griffith, V; Jha, AK: Critical Supply Shortage. The Need for Ventilators and Personal Protective Equipment During the Covid-19 Pandemic. —*The New England Journal of Medicine*, March 25, 2020. Accessed NEJM March 31, 2020

Robertson, Christopher T.; Rukavina, Mark; Fuse Brown, Erin C.: "New State Consumer Protections Against Medical Debt" —*The Journal of the American Medical Association*, 327(2): 121–122, 2022

Rosenbaum, Lisa: "Harnessing our Humanity — How Washington's Health Care Workers Have Risen to the Pandemic Challenge" —*The New England Journal of Medicine*, 382(22): 2069–2071, 2020

Rourke, Elizabeth: "In Clinical Care, What Will Amazon Deliver?" —*The New England Journal of Medicine*, 385(20): 2801–2803, 2021

Rourke, Elizabeth J.: "Ten Years of Choosing Wisely to Reduce Low-Value Care" —*The New England Journal of Medicine*, 386(14): 1293–1295, 2022

Scheinker, David; Milstein, Arnold; Schulman, Kevin: "The Dysfunctional Health Benefits Market and Implications for US Employers and Employees" —*The Journal of the American Medical Association*, 327(4): 323–324, 2022

Shrank, William H.; Chernew, Michael E.; Navathe, Amol S.: "Hierarchical Payment Models – A Path for Coordinating Population and Episode-Based Payment Models" —*The Journal of the American Medical Association*, 327(5): 423–424

Sittig, Dean F.; Sengstack, Patricia; Singh, Hardeep: "Guidelines for US Hospitals and Clinicians on Assessment of Electronic Health Record Safety Using SAFER Guides" —*The Journal of the American Medical Association*, 327(8), 719–720

Sowell, Thomas: *Knowledge and Decisions* —Basic Books, NY, 1996

Stern, Stefan: "Five New Management Rules for a Post-Pandemic Age" —*Financial Times*, November 22, 2021 (accessed 11/30/2021)

Stockdale, James: *Thoughts of a Philosophical Fighter Pilot* —Hoover Institution Press, Stanford, CA, 1995

Stout, Somava S.; Simpson, Lisa A.; Singh, Praphjot: "Trust Between Health Care and Community Organizations" —*The Journal of the American Medical Association*, 322(2) 109–110, 2019

Tollen, Laura; Keating, Elizabeth; Weil Alan: "How Administrative Spending Contributes to Excess U.S. Health Spending" —*Health Affairs*, February 20, 2020 (accessed 11/6/2021)

Toussiant, John; Conway, Patrick; Shortell Stephen: "The Toyota Production System: What Does It Mean, and What Does It Mean for Health Care?" —*Health Affairs*, April 6, 2016 (accessed 11/17/2021)

Tucker, Anita L.; Heisler, W. Scott; Janisse, Laura D.; Richter, Christine: "Designed for Workarounds: A Qualitative Study of Hospitals' Internal Supply Chains" —*The Permanente Journal*, 18(3), 33, 2014

Vicker, G.: "What sets the goals of public health?" —*The New England Journal of Medicine*, 589–596, 1958

Wallace, Megan; Sharfstein, Joshua M.: "The Patchwork U.S. Public Health System" —*The New England Journal of Medicine*, 386(1): 1–4, 2022

Wesson, Donald E.; Lucey, Catherine R.; Cooper, Lisa A.: "Building Trust in Helath Systems to Eliminate Health Disparities" —*The Journal of the American Medical Association*, 322(2): 111–112, 2019

Weinstein, Debra F.: "Reengineering GME in a Pandemic — Looking Back, and Forward" —*The New England Journal of Medicine*, 386(2): 97–99, 2022

Werner, Rachel M.; Glied, Sherry A.: "Covid-Induced Changes in Healthcare Delivery – Can They Last?" —*The New England Journal of Medicine*, 385(10): 868–870, 2001

Willink, Amber; Davis, Karen: "Coverage of Dental, Vision, and Hearing Services in Medicare: The Window of Opportunity is Open" —*The Journal of the American Medical Association*, 326(15): 1475–1476, 2021

Zhu, Jane M.; Polsky, Daniel: "Private Equity and Physician Medical Practices —Navigating a Changing Ecosystem" —*The New England Journal of Medicine*, 384(11): 981–983, 2021

Made in the USA
Monee, IL
08 April 2024